But for the Grace

But for the Grace

Profiles in Peace from a Nation at War

James A. Mitchell

Mansion Field

Published by
Mansion Field
an imprint of
Zeticula
57 St Vincent Crescent
Glasgow
G3 8NQ
Scotland

http://www.mansionfield.co.uk
admin@mansionfield.co.uk

ISBN-10 1-905021-11 9 Paperback
ISBN-13 978-1-905021-11 6 Paperback

To the people of Grace:

PEACE

சமாதானம்

සාමය

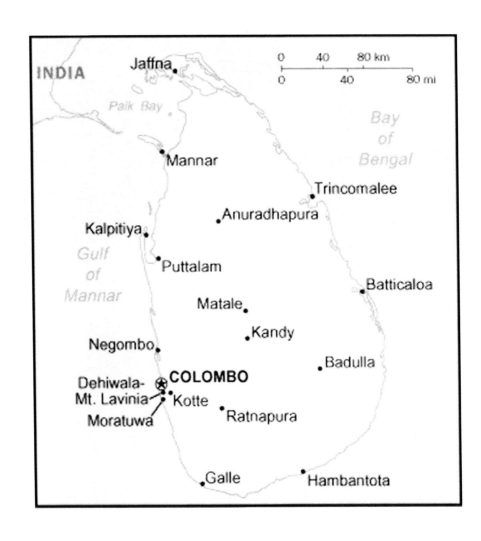

Foreword

Although Sri Lanka is probably my favourite place in the world, I think it is also one of the saddest. When I first arrived in Sri Lanka, some thirteen years ago, the place seemed so comfortable and familiar to me that I felt I had been there before; of course, my Buddhist friends told me that was because I had.

Reading these pages, my own memories of Trincomalee, Muttur and Nilaveli, on the island's east coast, return all too vividly. A place of inordinate beauty, the seemingly all pervasive smiles can, in a single black moment, be quite swept away. The capacity for violence in a land of general geniality is stunning to the outsider. Sri Lanka is often referred to as a tropical paradise. Alas, it is a deeply fractured paradise.

James Mitchell writes affectionately, and not a little movingly, about the extraordinary work and achievements at the Grace Care Center, north of Trinco. The difficulties of working in the area have meant that it has been largely abandoned by the agencies of outside assistance and this book tells a real success story for a change. It also gives the best account I have read anywhere of the brutality of abduction and life in an LTTE training camp for child soldiers.

The best thing about this book is that it is not judgemental. It graphically conveys to us all the horrors of war without feeling the need to point fingers. This book may even enrich the reader if it serves to convey the message propounded by one of the participants in the Grace Care Center, "Life is not about what surrounds you, it's about who you're surrounded by."

Paul Harris
February 2009

Paul Harris is the author of Delightfully Imperfect: A Year in Sri Lanka at the Galle Face Hotel *(Kennedy & Boyd 2006) and* Fractured Paradise: Images of Sri Lanka *(Frontline 2001) His autobiography* More Thrills than Skills: Adventures in Journalism, War and Terrorism *is published by Kennedy & Boyd (2009).*

With Appreciation
Acknowledgments

Over the years, Eric Parkinson heard countless proposals to help the Grace Care Center orphanage. The VeAhavta president entertained ideas from the practical to the wild, from the well-meaning to the 'just not happening.' When I told him I wanted to write a book about the orphanage, and what it offered to those who called it "home," he answered with characteristic brevity and honesty: "That would be great."

This was no small matter of trust. Eric protected Grace with absolute dedication, and I was honored that he allowed me to write this story. Eric: A grateful Grasshopper hopes this effort lives up to your expectations. You have inspired so many with such a simple idea: You can't save the world, but you can help make a small part of it a little better. You have, sir, in more ways than you may know.

Eric wasn't alone in his journey, and neither was this author. A long list of friends, colleagues, travel companions and others gave their time, thoughts and insights to make this project possible. In true story-telling tradition, we'll start at the beginning.

I was working for a suburban weekly newspaper when a man named Cliff Holbeck suggested that the community respond to the tsunami of Dec. 26, 2004 with a collective effort to help one particular cause. His daughter, Bailey, had been pen-pals with a girl in Sri Lanka; after the disaster, Cliff searched the Internet for agencies with connections to the island nation, and learned about VeAhavta, and Ann Arbor Dr. Naresh Gunaratnam, who was planning an early February mission to Trincomalee.

Included in the "South Lyon to Sri Lanka" campaign was having this reporter join Gunaratnam's team. Editor Sam Black and Publisher Rich Perlberg accepted and supported this idea, and the small community of South Lyon proved why it's called the "heartland" by contributing more than $20,000 to the orphanage – funds I was able to see put to use first-hand. Since that initial trip, people at the South Lyon Herald continued to support the idea of Grace, and my continued involvement: Darlene Herman (always first to volunteer); Deb Taylor (your artistry rocks); Phil Allmen, Dan Trudeau, Aly Iott and Nathan Mueller, at various times, did my job while I was out of the office (either physically or those many days when my mind was on the other side of the planet); and Nicole Stone (thanks, Bug Lady), Ray Dryer, Mayor John Doyle and many others helped us all learn that a small town's borders aren't as limited as some might think. The people of South Lyon formed a cross-planetary connection more inspiring than they may know. (And, of course, Mitch Ryder put some rock and roll into the campaign, and my career.)

On the home front, my parents, Eldon and Ruby Mitchell, Linda Remilong (the best person I've ever met), and my son, Alex, in turn encouraged, supported and accepted this Quixotic, mid-life crisis of mine that truly changed my life.

After four visits to Grace, my travel companions included many who invited new definitions of the word "hero." Working for peace in a combat zone tends to bring out the best in people, and my friends and colleagues sure had the right stuff to begin with. Naresh Gunaratnam (do I finally get a room in the monastery, Monk Dude?) gets the VeAhavta medal for patience for leading more than a dozen souls through that first post-tsunami trip. On that journey, (Dr. Auntie) Cheryl Huckins and Gina (What's up, Doc) Amalfitano began their long-term commitment that resulted in Mercy Home; you guys should have a coconut tree or something named in your honor. Risa Sharpe, Mohammad "Nadeem" Nadeemullah, Bonnie Sowa, Lynn Helland and others trusted me with their stories, and I pray, my dear friends, that my words captured the intended respect. Thanks to all of the World's Strangest Rock Band on Tour.

Also from South Lyon, middle school teacher Erin Whaley joined the journey when she made her first trip (of many) to Grace in August 2005. On that adventure Erin met her "Wonder Twin," Diane

McLaughlin. Our ongoing communications (while our lives changed so much around us) included your trust and confidence in this project. Di: You, my friend, are the 'rock star' among us; Erin: From Wonder Twin to Wonder Mom, you go, girl. Quite a crew we had, guys, in or out of the Indian Ocean. Thanks, Alex, for learning to do foreign correspondent work overnight, and for not stepping on any land mines. Tara and Kerrie: Let's go for a boat ride again someday.

This story of the orphanage, and the community of Trincomalee, couldn't have been told without the kind – often brave – assistance of many individuals in Sri Lanka. Lloyd Anthony Lorio's compassion and courage deserve a book of their own. Thank you, Father, for everything: You are a remarkable man. Amazing individuals met through Fr. Lorio include Sylvester Vasanthan, who taught me more than a few things about dignity and courage. Dr. Sathaharan Sundarlingam's friendship can be found on many pages in this book, just as lives at Grace were improved by his presence.

I owe a special nod, in oh-so-many ways, to Hiram Labrooy. You know what, pal? I'm actually unable to find the words to explain the help you've given this project, and its author, over the many miles we traveled. You are arguably the strangest human being I could ever hope (or fear) to meet, my friend, and this project simply couldn't have been done without you, just as Grace is what it is largely because of you.

The operations in Trinco and Batticaloa are little miracles of hope, and Rev. Selvadurai Jeyanesan, Rev. J. Gnanapragasm and Mr. Leonard David deserve more than a little credit for that. Thanks for showing me the crocodiles, Rev. Gnana; and Mr. David, I hope you know that your successes far outweigh any that you couldn't save. Too many people owe you their lives for you to think otherwise. Thank you, gentleman, for making my "solo flight" hardly a solitary journey.

Interviews for this book ranged from formal to casual, from questions asked of strangers who welcomed me into their homes to conversations held with people who became friends. To Angela, Denzia, Peter, Daisy and others on the Grace staff; there isn't a five-star hotel in the world that can make a guest feel as welcome as you folks. Mr. V. Yogeswaran, attorney, greatly helped my Sri Lankan education, as did Fr. Harry Miller in Batticaloa, Buddhist orphanage manager Kamamaldeniye Pamgnabissa, and retired Sri Lankan Supreme Court Justice C.V. Vigneswaran. I hope my work served you gentlemen with proper respect. Throughout Trinco, fishermen and people of the villages gave me their time whenever possible. Anandaperice, a justice of the peace and head of a fishing union, echoed the perspective of others I spoke with, providing a look at Trinco from atop the waves that both threatened and sustained a region. Thank you, gentlemen, for the time (and an incredible boat ride on the Indian Ocean). Kunam, from the Alles Gardens camp, introduced me to his friends and neighbors, and opened doors that this book desperately needed to include. A "home," I learned, is more than just solid walls.

At Mercy Home, Chandradasa – "Mr. Gandhi" – will not be forgotten, and this humble writer owes a world of gratitude to that kind man, and to dear Valliamma, for reliving a nightmare unimaginable without having been learned through tragic experience. The elders who made Mercy Home a community of dignity offer a lesson no history book can equal, and I thank them for allowing me to share moments of their time.

There are those who shared their thoughts and histories with me who must remain anonymous. Their tales are similar to the ones told in this volume; each individual tragedy reflects thousands of other untold histories.

All of these individuals helped me complete this book, but the true inspiration was as it should be: The "Grace Girls," the children who truly turned seven beaten acres into a vibrant, flourishing, peaceful place to call "Home." Some I came to know by name – Ushna, Ramiya, Nishantini, Sayanthini, Satheka, Danushi, Kovinthini, Tharshala – and others whose proper names my limited language couldn't quite master, but the recognition of a smile was a more-than-equal substitute. If your generation is the future of Sri Lanka, there remains hope for your beautiful island. To all the Grace children, my parting words from February 2008 remain true: I've been around a block or two in my life, but Grace Care Center is the most special place I've ever seen in the whole world, and it's because of you young ladies.

Thanks, girls: Anyone up for another sea bath?

Contents

State of Grace: Close Encounters in the Third World 255
VeAhavta volunteers explain the connection found, relationships formed and how those efforts may help provide a future for the children of Grace Care Center.

Oh, a storm is threatening
My very life today
If I don't get some shelter
Lord, I'm gonna fade away
War … children … is just a shot away.
– "Gimme Shelter," Jagger/Richards

Prologue

War Stories from the Mouths of Babes

When the war started back up, two women huddled in a small room with the youngest girls. One, a Michigan schoolteacher, was on her third visit to the children's home; the other, a social worker from Ohio, had been living at the orphanage for eight months.

In August 2006, the sounds of bombs and gunshots, attacks and retaliations were routinely heard near the orphanage. The children listened as the renewed war surrounded Trincomalee, Sri Lanka, the northeast port town long pivotal to the nation's struggles. For several days, no more than 10 minutes passed without the sound of one explosion or another.

The latest clash between the Government of Sri Lanka and the Liberation Tigers of Tamil Eelam targeted the village of Muttur to the south, and a Tiger compound just north of the Grace Care Center orphanage. It wasn't the first time the war was held in their backyard; it wouldn't be the last time they were caught in the crossfire.

The two women – strangers a year earlier, now the closest of friends – offered precious comfort to the youngest children, orphans of war or poverty. News reports about the situation asked if the 2002 cease-fire agreement still held; inside the orphanage, there was little question about whether or not the country was at war.

Diane McLaughlin (left) and Erin Whaley during a visit to the historic
Tiru Koneswaram, a Hindu temple in Trincomalee, with Grace Care Center
friends Tharshala, Nishantini and Suvinsala. Northeast Sri Lanka combines
both centuries-old monuments of peace and worship with the scars from
long-standing conflicts, often found in the same location.

On the first night of shelling, a dozen or so children sat in the room of Diane McLaughlin, a social worker from Cleveland. A year earlier, McLaughlin made a two-week trip to Grace before, a few months later, moving in for what was supposed to be a one-year stay as the facility's in-residence manager.

Inside the small but comfortable room, the recorded voices of Eric Parkinson and his wife, Sharon, were heard, reading bed-time stories in careful, loving English. Parkinson, a California attorney, helped establish the orphanage in 2002, the year the cease-fire agreement teased a suffering nation with hopes for peace. McLaughlin played the recorded stories, and a phone call allowed Parkinson to speak with some of the children.

"They were so cute," Parkinson said. "They told me all about the bombing sounds." War stories from the mouths of babes.

As reliable news sources, the children's reports weren't always accurate. During a particularly intense period of shelling, one girl counted the explosions and asked McLaughlin to confirm her math.

"Three bombs, Auntie?" she asked.

"Three is the only English number she knows," McLaughlin said. "It was more like sixty bombs."

Communications via 21st Century technology redefined "anachronism" in Trincomalee, which ranked among the world's most impoverished regions. Sri Lanka's northeast coast was overlooked by industrial age advancements until late into the 20th Century; cell phones and ox carts are equally familiar sights.

There was nothing high-tech about the war, however, which had mostly been fought the old-fashioned way. The result was the same; deaths are equally final whether caused by machete or laser-guided missile. Explosive weapons are timeless, as are the ethnic, religious or political divisions that create war.

For the people caught in the middle, it didn't really matter who fired the bullets or swung the machetes, or why. McLaughlin did her best to comfort the younger children, who wondered what the loud

War and peace: Barely a year after the Indian Ocean tsunami of Dec. 26, 2004, troops and armored personnel carriers (above) were a common sight in Trincomalee. In February 2006, false hopes again visited town (below) that peace would return to Sri Lanka, a wish held in spite of the renewed conflict.

bangs and booms meant; she offered sympathy to the older girls – who were all-too familiar with the sounds being heard.

"We are seriously under attack," McLaughlin described the situation. Early reports counted 32 fatalities in the region on the first day – some soldiers, a few Tigers, two men at a church not far from Grace, and a civilian who earned his living driving a three-wheel taxi known as a "tuk-tuk." The days, and the casualties, continued.

In the small room that McLaughlin now called "home," the family that had formed between some brave little girls and their American friends struggled to find peace in a nation at war. Parkinson spoke with the girls, hearing voices that didn't require translation for the message to be understood.

"It's hard for me to tell them apart from their high, squeaky voices," Parkinson said, although he clearly recalled the words of one particular girl. "Just before she passed the phone back to Diane, she said, 'I love you, Appa.' Such a sweetheart."

Three weeks later, Parkinson made yet another visit to the orphanage he'd established – far from his first, certainly not to be his last. As with the tsunami less than two years earlier, the return to war made an impossible dream harder still.

Encounters

Nilaveli Beach and the Happy Monkey

We were in a three-wheel taxi known, with affection, as a "tuk-tuk," little more than a golf cart that bounced along dodging bicycles, cows, other tuks, and the pothole-filled inconsistency of pavement torn by frequent use and limited maintenance.

Destruction took many forms in Sri Lanka, from the skeletons of bombed-out buildings to uprooted trees recently blasted out of their earthly sockets. A country both beautiful and broken, it was difficult to know which scars were from the recent tsunami, and which were the wounds of a 20-year war.

In spite of our surroundings, Eric Parkinson, a soft-spoken attorney from California, traded jokes with me as our tuk-tuk rocked, rolled and swayed its way back to the orphanage he'd helped create three years earlier. Grace Care Center was one facility of its kind in a community desperately in need of more. We'd seen images both tragic and comical (thus the trading of jokes), a morbid mixture not uncommon in harsh elements. On the northeast coast, Trincomalee was among the pivotal regions in Sri Lanka's civil conflict; it also hosted some of the widest-spread, harshest poverty in the world.

On December 26, 2004, a bad situation was made worse. One of history's deadliest natural disasters – the Indian Ocean tsunami – was not the worst thing to ever happen to many Sri Lankans. Parkinson called it, "Par for the course," in the lives of the orphan children: Just another lousy day in paradise.

Five weeks after the disaster, Parkinson was back – again – at Grace, a residence with more than 100 children, survivors of poverty or war. On the final day of a hurried trip, there were two things he wanted to do before leaving Trinco; he extended a casual invitation.

"Wanna take a walk?" he asked. I had few specific plans for my second morning at the orphanage, other than recovering from the 48-hour door-

to-door trip. The obvious sense of urgency felt by our group of volunteers was balanced by an aspect of the culture often described as, "Lanka time," a relaxed pace where appointments are more approximate than determined. It was a peaceful place, in spite of the harsh realities that dominate its landscape.

Our first stop was not far. The orphanage, which sat on seven acres of beachfront property, was enclosed by a cinderblock wall topped with embedded shards of broken glass (a perimeter equally discouraging to animals or those who consider young girls a commodity). The adjacent field housed one of the region's many camps for Internally Displaced Persons, refugees in their own land who lost their homes to war or catastrophe. Known as Alles Gardens, more than two-dozen families formed a makeshift, struggling community. They had so little before the tsunami; they now had less.

Parkinson walked the length of the camp, speaking (through an interpreter) with the residents, his video recorder capturing the uneven rows of patchwork huts, partial tents and lean-to's. A child swung happily on an improvised swing: A length of rope was looped over an improbable frame of sturdy tree branches; somehow (without having much of a tool selection) the men sunk the poles deep enough to withstand an aggressive child's play. The adults simply wanted to give the kids something – anything – to take their minds off the tsunami: The children didn't like to play on the beach anymore.

The camp's residents were, in fact, half of the pre-tsunami community that found a home there after theirs was lost to the war. Those who left were fishermen no longer able to make their living from the sea after their boats were destroyed by the pounding waves. The shores of Trinco were littered with ruptured vessels that could no longer feed a population. Several of the shelters were supported or reinforced with pieces of broken boat.

After touring the camp, Parkinson's next stop was 10 kilometers north of the orphanage. A few years earlier, the Mauro Beach hotel near Nilaveli Beach was Parkinson's home-away-from-home when he scouted properties for Grace. Parkinson wanted to see how the hotel fared against the tsunami, the extent of which would not be known for some time. More than 200,000 souls were killed by the immediate impact; 40,000 from Sri Lanka's

In the aftermath of the December 2004 tsunami, VeAhavta founder and President Eric Parkinson toured a shattered hotel in Nilaveli Beach, which served as Parkinson's home-away-from-home while scouting properties for the Grace Care Center orphanage he established in 2002.

There but for the Grace: Created by war or disaster, Sri Lanka's eastern coast includes thousands of makeshift camps (above), populated by families of desperate relatives clinging together. One such camp (below) borders the seven-acre Grace Care Center orphanage and church, an island of hope in a struggling land.

struggling population of 19 million. It was impossible to know how many hundreds of thousands of families were made homeless in mere seconds.

Our hired tuk-tuk could only get as far as a side road leading toward the hotel; the wreckage required completing the journey on foot. We walked through piles of bricks, stepped around knocked-over trees with eight-foot-wide root balls, and crawled over the walls of the hotel. (About 180 guests and staff were at the resort when the tsunami hit; 60 survived.)

At what used to be the ocean-side gate of the hotel, Parkinson communicated with workers just starting the daunting task of rebuilding their livelihood. A sympathetic, sincere smile spoke volumes, no matter the language barrier. They pointed skyward to illustrate the heights of the waves; they could point in any direction to explain the damage.

Before heading back to the tuk-tuk, Parkinson invited me for another walk, with no destination other than a stroll up the beach. Little was said, as both "Lanka Time" and our surroundings took hold: The beach gave way to the jungle's edge, a tree line rearranged (but unbeaten) by nature. The ocean's splash and roar were joined by an occasional snapped twig, the sound of an animal or, from above, the cawing of crows searching the sands for food.

"I love this country," Parkinson said. It's a multi-faceted love affair, from the physical charms of its natural beauty to the hearts and soul of its people; the blissful innocence of children whose worldview included a lifelong, front-row seat to a civil war.

"How long you going to do this," I asked.

"Long as I can, I guess," he answered, not trying to qualify the statement, not hesitating to speak honestly.

In many ways, Sri Lanka was an island of extremes, from the massive extent of poverty and disaster to the sheer, blinding beauty of its beaches, jungles, culture and people. It was also filled with light-hearted reminders of life's simplest – sometimes strangest – pleasures.

We walked past the sagging fence that bordered the hotel's courtyard, which a group of monkeys had seemingly claimed. A few dozen animals lounged on upended patio furniture that wouldn't seat human guests again for months. We stopped to take pictures: One notable creature crouched, facing slightly away from us, on a branch just a few feet from the fence.

I climbed a nearby mound of broken concrete, and zoomed in for a portrait. My viewfinder was filled with primate and tree, and it promised to be an interesting picture.

As my finger prepared to press the button, the monkey pivoted to face me. The erection he sprouted seemed – at the time – to be pointed at me like a loaded pistol. A real "Kodak moment," to be sure.

We were still laughing at the image, several kilometers away, while riding past a camp belonging to the Liberation Tigers of Tamil Eelam, the armed group of either freedom fighters or terrorists, depending on who was keeping score. We traded juvenile, silly jokes, and considered creative plans for the picture I took, ranging from use as a screen saver to postcards for tourism: Welcome to Sri Lanka, Baby!

"Good to know the tsunami didn't upset the local wildlife too much," I said. "Think 'National Geographic' might pay me for this?"

"Happy little bugger," Parkinson laughed. The jokes ended soon, reality again taking center stage as we drew close to Grace Care Center and its perpetual cycle of motion and life. Since welcoming the first 10 girls in 2002, the population grew to more than 100 children; programs were added as funding became available, with more being considered. When Grace first opened, Parkinson had reason for cautious optimism: That same month, a cease-fire agreement was reached between the Government of Sri Lanka and the Tamil Tigers. Trinco, as the town was known, was a perfect location for Grace to flourish. Parkinson believed he and the nonprofit group he founded could bring Grace to a point where it was funded, mostly self-sufficient, and he could, "Turn over the keys and find something else to do."

The tsunami washed away that thought. In the months and years that followed the disaster, the failed cease-fire and escalated war would make just keeping the orphanage in existence a constant struggle. The community Grace called home – which often served as a battleground in the ongoing war – was a delicate mix of contradictions: A short morning's drive encountered rebel camps, refugee communities, fields filled with landmines, prayer stations of several faiths, and wildlife adapting to their environment.

Welcome to Sri Lanka, baby.

First they came for the Communists,
but I was not a Communist so I did not speak out.
Then they came for the Socialists and the Trade Unionists,
but I was neither, so I did not speak out.
Then they came for the Jews,
but I was not a Jew so I did not speak out.
And when they came for me,
there was no one left to speak out for me.
– Martin Niemoeller (1892-1984)

Chapter 1
The Ballad of Eric-Uncle and Rev. Jey

It was easy to fall for the children he met: "Cute" doesn't begin to describe the unbridled joy in the small faces, happy as only infants can be, smiling their way through poverty and war, having never known comfort or peace.

Eric Parkinson became acquainted with several children early into his Sri Lankan journey. In one specific instance – and he freely admits it sounds strange to say – he thought he saw something familiar.

"I was playing tag with the kids and picked one of them up," Parkinson said. Child and man laughed together; their faces flushed with playtime smiles. "I know it sounds weird, but I swear I saw my son's eyes."

Parkinson shrugged. Believe it; don't believe it, maybe you just had to be there. He doesn't push the point when describing the memory. So many stories in northeast Sri Lanka were very much a case of: You have to see it to believe it.

It was a passing moment, but one that brought a sad, tragic perspective to the curious mission he'd started. Seeing familiar eyes transposed onto a strange child's face wasn't, by itself, a defining moment; it simply confirmed a path already chosen.

"It didn't seem fair. One kid gets born into this color skin with all these advantages, and another child gets born with … nothing," Parkinson said. "How are these decisions made? Who makes them? The children certainly weren't consulted. You can go crazy with questions like this."

***

Sri Lanka was something of an accidental destination, an unexpected discovery as much as a mission. In early 2000, Parkinson was a 38-year-old attorney practicing civil law in southern California. He and his wife, Sharon, were parents of an infant son – and would soon add a daughter to the family.

Parkinson's circle of friends included Joseph Frankovic, a biblical scholar studying Midrash (the interpretation of Jewish texts) at Jerusalem's Hebrew University. Frankovic's lessons came from David Flusser, credited as being among the first Israeli's to study ancient texts in search of Christianity's Jewish roots. While in the Holy Land, Frankovic came to know a minister from the Church of South India, a union of four protestant traditions (Anglican, Congregational, Presbyterian and Methodist) formed in 1947 under the motto, "That they all may be one." By the end of the 20th Century the church had nearly 4 million members in 21 dioceses, 20 in India and one, the diocese of Jaffna, in Sri Lanka.

Frankovic raved to Parkinson about the near-legends he'd heard about Rev. Salvaduri Jeyanesan, a 50-year-old cleric originally from Sri Lanka's northernmost Jaffna peninsula. Frankovic raved to Parkinson about this ambitious minister.

"He said, 'You gotta meet this guy,'" Parkinson recalled. "'He's incredible, doing amazing work. He thinks like a Jew.'"

Jeyanesan was ordained in 1978 after training throughout the decade at Indian seminaries. The year before his certification, he'd married his wife, Shantha, and the couple would raise two children, Dushy and Niran, the younger boy who, in 1986, lost a kidney to a landmine explosion. When the children were of sufficient age, they joined a growing migration to India, which was becoming increasingly populated with Tamils seeking an escape from the conflict. (Niran eventually joined the growing Tamil community in Toronto, Canada. Dushy is studying nursing in New York.)

Many clerics in the country joined the civilians who left Sri Lanka, but 'Rev. Jey,' as Parkinson came to know him, remained commited to his work, based in the eastern town Batticaloa, where in 1989 he established St. John's Center to provide assistance to children and women suffering from the ongoing civil conflict.

By the early 21ˢᵗ Century Jeyanesan was a frequent traveler, raising funds for his mission and continuing his education, which included the Midrash teachings being studied by Parkinson's American friend. The lessons meant more than finding a historical context for his faith, but helped guide his contemporary efforts.

"Jey's theological horizons were greatly expanded," Parkinson said. "He learned that Jesus was a Jewish sage who spoke and taught almost exclusively to other Jews, not to gentiles; because of this, his sayings would only make sense when viewed from within the Hebraic context. It was a real eye-opener for Jey."

In other ways, Parkinson's own worldview broadened the more he learned about Jeyanesan, and Sri Lanka, where a 20-year war and devastating poverty in the northeast created nothing less than a humanitarian crisis. Few American were familiar with the seemingly isolated problems on the other side of the world, let alone thought that they could be of assistance. Parkinson was impressed by the hands-on approach that Jeyanesan applied: By then, St. John's operated five orphanages and managed and supplied several feeding centers.

Inspired to lend assistance to the effort, Parkinson helped arrange a six-city North American speaking tour, where in early 2001 the Third World minister appeared before civic groups, churches and anyone else they could find. Jey's tour began near Los Angeles, not far from Parkinson's San Luis Obispo home.

In contrast to the life Jeyanesan had lived, the energetic, smiling minister surprised Parkinson from the moment they met.

Eric Parkinson with Grace Care Center staff members Dharshini (left) and Susinthe, young women who helped supervise 100-plus children. The contract to purchase the Grace property was signed during the same month that the Government of Sri Lanka and the Liberation Tigers of Tamil Eelam entered into a cease-fire agreement.

"I'll never forget the day I picked him up at the airport," Parkinson said. "I thought he would be the saddest, most broken guy; he'd seen so much hardship in the world. I expected someone whose soul would have been darker."

Instead, Parkinson welcomed a beaming man, "Full of joy." From their initial meeting, Jeyanesan's dedication impressed the attorney.

"Something clicked, I hit it off with him right away," Parkinson said. With the tenacity of a prospective lawyer cramming for the bar exam, Parkinson learned the tragedies of war from a man committed to helping its victims and survivors. They stayed up into the small hours of the morning talking and drinking tea (a new experience for Parkinson that would become a habit). They spoke of religion, of war and peace, of the difference between talking about doing something and actually getting the work done.

There was plenty to do, both in Batticaloa and, 100 kilometers to the north, in Trincomalee, the coastal town central to the conflict since its start. "Trinco" and its residents bore witness to religious and ethnic tensions with centuries-old roots. In the northeast, the biblical priority of helping widows and orphans was strongly in demand.

On the face of the planet, Sri Lanka itself seems an orphan, slightly adrift from India's southern tip, so close yet removed from the world around it. It's been called "India's tear drop" for its identifiable shape; named "Serendib" by Arab sailors who coined the phrase for, "Unexpected, pleasant surprise." Travelers from Marco Polo to Mark Twain to Arthur C. Clarke marveled at the riches and beauty of the former Ceylon, while admiring the simple elegance of its people.

The population, however, was not always harmonious, and ethnic tensions rose to the surface not long after the nation declared independence from its colonial rule. Division among ethnic groups was, at first, a political problem in the early decades of self-government; those debates became armed conflicts in the early 1980s.

The war, however, was just one of many challenges facing the small island nation, especially its youngest citizens. "In east Asia," Jeyanesan said, "child prostitution is a thriving business. It is into these places we must go. The church," he said, "is the only organization in the world that should care more about its non-members than it does its members. We must treat these orphaned children as though they were our own."

Living and preaching, working and serving in the embattled north and east, Jey cared little for the ethnic or religious origins of the conflict, and held no allegiance to the principal opponents in the battle: The Government of Sri Lanka and the Liberation Tigers of Tamil Eelam. The LTTE – known as the Tamil Tigers – were said to have started the war in 1983, with the ambush of an Army patrol near the south-eastern capital Colombo, the nation's largest city of nearly 1 million. Others claimed that decades of discrimination by the majority Sinhalese inspired the attack by the separatist group, who would develop a reputation as one of the world's leading terror organizations in their quest for a separate homeland for Tamils.

The stories told by Rev. Jey were not taken from scholarly texts or philosophical offerings, but from first-hand experience. His interests lay with the innocent civilians and children whose homes became someone else's battleground. The basic solutions he described – simply feeding and sheltering those who could not do so for themselves – made perfect sense to Parkinson.

"At the end of his trip, I told him that Sharon and I would like to help however we could," Parkinson said, expecting a request for funds and willing to oblige as much as possible.

It wasn't just money that was needed, Jeyanesan answered. Without hesitation, he told Parkinson: "Help us build a new orphanage."

***

The island nation Ceylon shed its colonial status in 1948 when it declared its separation from Great Britain. In 1972, a new constitution was signed for the Democratic Socialist Republic of Sri Lanka, a Singhalese name ("Great Land") in deference to the majority (74 percent) population. The island's second largest group, the minority Tamils, represented 18 percent of the population and lived mostly in the north and east.

As countries go, Sri Lanka is fairly small; its 19 million inhabitants sharing just over 25,000 square miles (a thousand more than the American state of West Virginia; about half the size of England). Very few Sri Lankans are lifelong residents of one village or another, as the years, decades and centuries tell tales of migration, relocation and evacuations. Family and civic histories contain ancient origins, as both Tamils and Singhalese established territories throughout the island as early as the 5th and 6th Century BCE, when Singhalese warriors conquered the nomadic Veddah tribes (considered to be the island's first settlers), and established kingdoms primarily in the south and west. Tamils – coming across from southern India – established their heritage mostly in the north and along the east coast; over the centuries, their number increased as Portuguese, Dutch and, British colonizers brought laborers in from the north. During its reign of oversight, Great Britain aggressively nurtured Ceylon into a significant exporter of tea, cinnamon and coconuts.

Most of Sri Lanka's populated areas were primarily either Singhalese or Tamil, an unofficial segregation firmly in place when independence was declared. Many felt that the freedom would allow for more integration, although tensions existed between the groups. Some Singhalese felt that they had been treated unfairly by previous rulers, who seemed to favor the Tamil people with more prominent opportunities. Tamils, in turn, objected to some of the decisions made as the country formed its first self-government with what seemed to be a bias in favor of Singhalese. Notably, Buddhism (the ethnic group's prominent religion) was constitutionally declared to have, "The foremost place" with respect to religion, and Sinhala was deemed the "official language" of Sri Lanka. Further, some argued that safeguards were eliminated for minorities by the same updated Constitution, and the largely Hindu Tamils often felt relegated to second-class citizenship.

Humble beginnings: The seven-acre Grace property (above) once housed a resort hotel that took advantage of the region's reputation for breathtaking beaches and challenging waves to surf. (Photo courtesy of Eric Parkinson.) Approaching the main hall a year later required passing by the Vocational Training Center (below) as the compound quickly put its plans into action.

Along the northeast coast, Trincomalee stood as an exception to Sri Lanka's segregation. Its population of nearly 322,000 held a rare, melting-pot mix of about one-third each Tamil, Singhalese and Muslim citizens. In that pivotal town, Rev. Jeyanesan envisioned a children's home, a desperately needed haven for those made orphans by war or poverty. The mix of ethnic and religious groups in Trinco offered a unique, cautious opportunity for success.

"It's a great place for something like this," Parkinson said. "It's also a dangerous place to try something like this. It's kind of a tinderbox."

The Grace Care Center, as envisioned by Parkinson and Rev. Jey, could offer safety and hope to children in need, regardless of ethnic origin or religious persuasion. Based on the model of St. John's, their dream was a home for 100 girls that could include vocational training as well as basic education. (They wouldn't have to search hard for eligible children; the north and east suffered a disproportionate number of the war casualties; the conflict left another 800,000 Sri Lankans destitute. Among those who hadn't lost their homes to poverty and conflict, an estimated 80 percent of families in Sri Lanka's northern regions lived well below even the most generous standard for poverty, surviving on less than $20 a month.)

By the time Parkinson went to Sri Lanka, he traveled alone, but with the support, encouragement and early funding of the organization he formed: The non-profit group VeAhavta took its name from the Hebrew verb meaning, "You shall love." The imperative – "You shall love others as you love yourself" (not unlike the Christian Golden Rule) – does not specify who shall be loved, nor offer reward for the love itself: The act is the important thing.

At first, Parkinson expected to simply hand over the money he raised and wish Jeyanesan well. That plan didn't last long: Jeyanesan said that Parkinson must see for himself, and arrangements were made for a trip to southern Asia.

Had Parkinson been looking for an excuse to cancel his plans, history offered one: The tickets purchased in August were for a flight in late September 2001. Family and friends asked him to reconsider after the Sept. 11 terrorist attacks on America forever changed a nation and world. Instead, Parkinson focused harder on his mission, all the more aware now of why the orphanage was so desperately needed. There was nothing he could do about Sept. 11; maybe he could do something about another problem.

Besides, Parkinson had given his word: Frankovic and Jeyanesan urged him to see the situation for himself, and he had agreed. Abandoning the yet-unknown children he could help was not an option. When flights were again cleared to depart from the United States, Parkinson traveled the 30 air hours between California and Sri Lanka, landing in Colombo and motoring another eight hours along narrow roads to the east coast.

Through his considerable contacts, Jeyanesan had selected three potential properties on the outskirts of Trinco, and a real estate scouting mission was conducted. The first two were not impressive. "Real dumps," Parkinson sighed, building an expectation that any available properties would be too war-torn or neglected to be viable.

A third one wasn't much better, the grounds of a small hotel on the beach just north of Trinco proper. They walked the property, shared greetings with local fishermen who lugged their boats and catch in and out of the Indian Ocean the old-fashioned way, with nets grudgingly lugged ashore by man-power.

They were ready to call it a day, when Frankovic saw something while exploring the hotel property.

"Joseph looked over the wall and said, 'Wow, look at that place,'" Parkinson said.

Several buildings stood strong against the sea air, although any use as a hotel had long been abandoned. There was something promising about the place, a vision that came to Parkinson as clear as when he saw the eyes of a child facing an uncertain future: A fairly well-defined seven acres that offered sufficient rise from the beach, fertile vegetation and access to the nearby road coming from Trinco.

There were problems, however. The property's owner moved to Madras in the early 1980s, when the war sparked increasing riots and hostilities throughout the island. The hotel had been abandoned since 1983; its seven neglected buildings untended victims of salt air, ocean winds and scavenging animals.

There was something about the place, though, and about the timing of opportunity. The owner, now the proprietor of a Singapore shipping company, was in Trinco that very week for a rare visit to his native land.

"Within an hour, we were walking the property with this guy," Parkinson said.

Real estate transactions are fairly universal. Parkinson spent a flattering hour being "buttered up" and praised by the land owner. Everyone was all smiles, until Parkinson asked what the going rate was for the seven beaten acres and fading buildings.

"He saw my skin color, and the price was very high," Parkinson said. "Like, $1.2 million. We laughed. I was very candid; told him we didn't have anything like that."

Negotiations continued long into the afternoon, the baking sun finally losing its 100-plus degree potency, the sound of the surf a constant wash over the proceedings. The price came down a bit, and Jeyanesan said how, "The Bishop himself" (with whom Parkinson and Jey had met the previous day) would be very pleased by the project.

The price finally dropped to $280,000. The local fishermen and villagers enthusiastically told Parkinson what a tremendous bargain he was being offered.

"You guys haven't been listening," Parkinson said. "I've got $20,000 – I can't possibly afford this."

"Don't worry about the money," Jeyanesan assured Parkinson. "God is not short of cash."

That's easy for you to say, Parkinson thought, but did not verbalize. He was imagining the day he would return home to tell his family, his wife, what he had done. "Guess what I bought, honey," he might say. (Sharon Parkinson would be supportive, of course, but stunned, as were Parkinson's friends.)

The day ended, however, with a deal having been made. Signatures on paper soon followed, confirming the commitment of a lifetime.

"Four days later, I was in Colombo signing this contract," Parkinson said. "I had severe 'Buyer's remorse.' I came real close to calling it off."

Instead, a $10,000 deposit was put down toward the purchase, with the promise of both completing the deal and building an orphanage in a third world region.

"I had no idea how we were going to do this," Parkinson said. Over the weeks that followed, funds were raised and efforts began to make the property suitable as a home for 100 children. A payment of $85,000 was needed – and raised – to satisfy engineering requirements. The December deadline for the balance of the property cost was approaching, and VeAhavta had not reached the needed amount.

The owner, however, was having tax problems, and asked that the payment be delayed until well into the following year.

Putting on a good show, Parkinson pretended to be disappointed: "Okay, we were ready, but we'll hold off," he told them. Fund-raising continued, and the property was beginning to resemble a welcoming home.

Parkinson's signature on purchasing papers that December wasn't the only official promise made in Sri Lanka that month. On Christmas Eve, a formal cease-fire agreement was signed by the LTTE and the Government of Sri Lanka, which now included the recently-elected Prime Minister Ranil Wickremesinghe. The truce was brokered by a Norwegian delegation, the Sri Lanka Monitoring Mission, a neutral panel of negotiators providing third-party oversight.

Even the skeptics saw reasons for hope. Verbal agreements had been made before, but not with as much formality or international monitoring. In early 2002, the cease-fire was renewed, and some dared hope that peace would again return to the land that promised 'serendipity.'

VeAhavta's overseas agent, Rev. S. Jeyanesan (above) addresses a ceremony at Grace Care Center. Eric Parkinson starts some counting lessons with a young Grace student; no matter how busy his schedules when visiting Grace, the VeAhavta president's time with the children confirmed the connection he made with a land, a people on the other side of the planet. (Photos by Sam Larkin.)

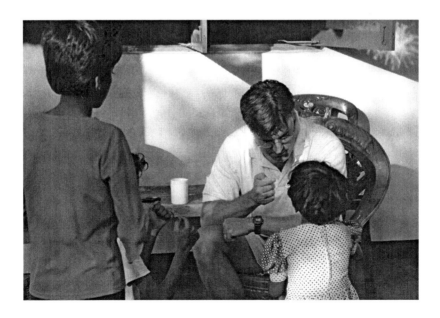

***

It wasn't just the children who inspired Parkinson. During an early visit to Sri Lanka, Parkinson learned of prisoners still in government custody in spite of the peace accord: Men kept in little more than cages for three years or more, some tortured, most treated less than human in a jail as close to being a medieval dungeon as Parkinson would ever see. They were held under the 1979-imposed Prevention of Terrorism Act, which offered the national police force near unlimited powers to arrest, and detain. ("Evidence," in a few cases Parkinson encountered, included signed "confessions" written in Sinhalese, a language that few Tamil prisoners could speak or read, let alone write.)

A group of 18 men were kept in a 25-square-foot cell, served a single daily meal of rice through a slot in the wall, and forced to live in their collective excrement. They were told, under the law, they could be confined for up to 18 months under court or police orders that were, "Final and shall not be called in question in any court or tribune." There were several exceptions that allowed the confinement to extend beyond that sentence.

Parkinson agreed to meet with a group of prisoners who had been held in custody beyond the proscribed time frame, long enough to have abandoned much hope. On Aug. 28, 2002, Parkinson, Rev. Jey and local attorney Chandran Chiniah spent two hours in the Batticaloa prison. He heard stories that haunted him, bringing forth images he would never forget:

"Imagine the eyes of a man who has been torn from his wife and children in the midst of war and all its uncertainties, imprisoned with 17 other men, suffered physical and mental torture, been looked down upon as 'inferior' by his captors. They are eyes of shock, hate, anxiety, hopelessness, humiliation, embarrassment and insecurity."

Parkinson was stunned by what he saw, and learned. Those arrested under the Prevention of Terrorism Act, he said, typically just "disappear" one day, leaving family members with no clues as to their whereabouts.

The most amazing thing, however, was in the dignity he found in a Draconian prison cell. VeAhavta and Parkinson agreed to work with Chiniah and finance representation for eight of the 18 men they met (funding the legal costs for the rest of the men became a VeAhavta priority that was soon fulfilled). A group of 18 desperate men were told that eight of them could be helped toward freedom.

Their response remains among his strongest memories Parkinson would have of the Sri Lankan people he met.

"Six men immediately stepped forward and told me to help someone other than themselves," Parkinson said. "They had neither wives nor children at home while some of the others did." The prisoners argued others' cases: one had a young wife who needed him; another had children.

Two of the men who lobbied for someone else had been in custody for more than three years, with little remaining expectation that they would ever be released.

"That just blew me away," said Parkinson. The eight men were released after just one court appearance (calling into question the severity of the non-charges under which they were held); the remaining 10 were released within nine months after Parkinson obtained additional funds.

When Parkinson left the Batticaloa prison, he breathed deeply to clear the smells of captivity from his lungs; he stretched his muscles, uncoiling the knots that seemed to have formed in his back, neck, shoulders. He realized how tense he had been throughout the entire visit, on edge during every minute he was inside.

"Maybe," he said, "I was concerned that getting into the prison would be easier than getting out."

***

On August 31, 2002, a ceremony was held on seven acres of beachfront, now called the Grace Care Center, offering the promise of a future. That same month, representatives from both the Tamil Tigers and Government of Sri Lanka sat, for the first time, to discuss a resolution to the conflict that had dominated the land for two decades.

"There was tremendous optimism everywhere about the cease fire," Parkinson said. Conversations at the opening of Grace Home were held between local officials and nearly two dozen ministers from the Church of South India, many of whom were making their first journey in years away from the northern, Tamil-dominated Jaffna peninsula.

Some of the first dozen girls to call the campus "home" were fresh from the battlefields that had framed their childhood. They called him "Eric-Uncle," a title of respect comparable to "Mister" that the children used to address their honored visitors.

Opening the orphanage was just the beginning. The obstacles seemed limitless, yet the vision, initially focused on a peaceful seven acres and 100 children to call it "home," was of the simple growth of helping a community to help itself. Every child, Parkinson thought, had a value and a choice, perhaps seen largest in a relatively small population, where villages could raise children and children could, one day, either save a village, or join a culture in its demise.

"I see it now as an opportunity, that's the way you have to look at it," Parkinson said. "In the Jewish tradition is this concept that, if you save a child, you save the world. You save that person's world. Their world is as important to them as your world is to you."

The world of the children at Grace Care Center was not, he admitted, a pretty place.

"These kids have spent their entire lives in war," Parkinson said. "They've never known any other reality. They saw their parents butchered in front of them, their mothers raped." Parkinson would, sometimes, ask himself: "Who makes those decisions," that one child lived a certain way and another is subjected to a life of inhumanity.

Born in 2001, Rurendra Darshika, seen here during a morning visit to
Mercy Home, attended the Grace Day Care program, where she enjoyed
signing and playing sports with the other children. The program provided
up to 60 local, pre-school-age children with early education, two daily meals
and a cool place for an afternoon nap, allowing their parents to work, if or
when employment could be found.

Even 'Tough Chicks' Cry

It's hard not to like a girl who tries to make people smile – laugh, if possible – even through tragedies like the tsunami.

That was my introduction to "Sundari," a spirited, handful of a child a year away from her 16th birthday. If personality were measured in pounds, her outgoing, outspoken presence far outweighed her small frame. The transition from rowdy "tom boy" into graceful young lady is a challenge under the best of circumstances; hers were a long way from being the best of anything.

Give that girl an audience, though, and she'll play it for laughs. In honor of Eric Parkinson's last night at Grace Care Center in February 2005, the children staged a talent show of dances, songs and poems of a topical nature, somber rhymes dedicated to the victims and survivors of the tsunami.

The show also featured a short, comic play, seeking amusement in spite of the harsh realities. At center stage, Sundari guided several girls through a prepared scene. The dialogue was not in a language we understood, but the physical comedy and laughter of children came through loud and clear. The plot was often interrupted by miscues, forgotten lines, and the predictable onstage giggles heard at any school pageant.

For those of us who only recently met the girls, it was a chance to see which of the little clowns stood out from the crowd. Among them, Sundari was easily noticed; satiric comedy always makes a presence.

It's not that Sundari wasn't upset by the disaster; she was all-too familiar with life's most brutal tragedies. She was serious when needed, as when serving as "group leader" to eight younger children. As rowdy as they come – still a rough-and-tumble child at heart – to her small group Sundari was stern, loving, watchful. The little ones looked up to her, for good reason: A gentle big sister not above barking out orders during after-school chores.

"You're a real bossy little thing, aren't you?" I asked after she shepherded a group off the bus with obvious marching orders for the afternoon.

"Awww," the bossy little thing disappeared in a blush, her almond eyes twinkled a smile.

"Sure, a real 'tough chick,'" I joked, a specific translation unnecessary.

She wasn't so tough, not really, even though she had to be on more than one occasion. Sundari survived a harsh, challenging life with few (serious) complaints; when you don't know that a better, peaceful existence is possible, there's no reason to cry about what you don't have.

Not to say she couldn't be a handful, even a petulant child. During a visit in early 2006, Parkinson e-mailed me a photo he'd taken of Sundari, a candid moment where she appeared about to say something to someone off-camera, an exasperated look on her face. Parkinson described the picture as her, "I'm getting ready to whine" expression. (A frequent moment during her early days at Grace, I was often told.) After a quick translation, Sundari understood the teasing joke, offered with love and affection.

The photo was sent to help cheer up the patient. A few days earlier, Sundari injured her arm on the playground at school, a minor accident during a game of "net ball" (a put-the-ball-through-a-hoop contest not unlike basketball, only without a backboard). The improvised sling she'd been given – a length of gauze tied around her neck that (sort of) held her forearm stable – made our evening routine a bit of a challenge. The dining room at Grace Home hosted a dozen lengthy tables, each seating eight to 10 girls. At each meal, Sundari saw me coming, and made a procedure out of vacating her place at the table's head for me. That night, she bravely used her one good arm to slide children and plates to the side.

While trying to help rearranging the seating, I bumped into her cradled arm. She didn't yell, or cry, but she inhaled sharply and clenched her teeth as if in severe pain. It seemed to be more than the simple sprain she'd been told it was, and I walked her over to the clinic. Our group included, as always, a doctor, who confirmed my layman's diagnosis that additional medical attention, including an x-ray, was needed.

We loaded Sundari into a van and headed for Trincomalee General Hospital. It was a mostly silent ride through a darkened Trinco, occasional

In northeast Sri Lanka, young girls are among the most vulnerable in the world, whether from the region's child slavery traffic or as potential soldiers in the ongoing war. It remains unknown how many children have been conscripted by the Liberation Tigers of Tamil Eelam or, as many charge, in equal number by paramilitary organizations supported by the Government of Sri Lanka. Children as young as 10 have been drafted into service; teenage girls have been sent on suicide bomb missions.

Be it ever so humble: In the small kitchen area, the staff at Grace Care Center produces three meals a day for up to 100 children. (Below) Compared to the scenery of Trinco just outside its gates, visitors unanimously describe the sense of serenity on the orphanage grounds. In The Children's Park, "True peace allows children the freedom to be children."

fires and lanterns illuminated small roadside circles in the villages surrounding town. Men gathered in front of closed shops to play cards, their game lit by steel drums that burned the days' debris. The cows had settled on the beach or in fields for the night, and dogs of indeterminate breed prowled the streets for some nocturnal scavenging. The security forces were nearly invisible, watching from the shadows of trees or sandbagged bunkers.

Sundari didn't cry, even when poked and prodded by doctors before an x-ray confirmed a nasty fracture to her forearm. A more suitable sling was found for her arm, now properly wrapped in a tight bandage, and she was given a prescription to help ease some of her physical pain.

Sundari's English was limited, but gestures and body language filled in any conversational gaps, whether determining if a doctor was needed or just hanging around at Grace Care Center. No translation was needed, for example, in a staring contest, with victory belonging to whoever went unblinking the longest. We matched eyes for minutes on end, and I "won" each competition until the last one, the day before we left Grace. She was determined to outlast me during a final challenge, a goal that, once reached, was celebrated with a joyous, beaming smile that revealed her true age.

All in all, she wasn't such a "touch chick," as seen when we said our good-byes the next day. She lingered on the perimeter of our group's farewells with the kids, elders, staff and friends; Sundari drifted off, into the main hall where I found her standing in a corner, hugging herself, trying to hide the tears in her unblinking eyes.

It took a lot to make that kid cry. (Hers were hardly the only tears shed during that good-bye scene.) She knew how pointless it was, a lesson learned while growing up in one of the most impoverished regions in the world, or from becoming an orphan at age 10, or from seeing the tsunami destroy countless homes and families.

Maybe because she had to grow up earlier, harder, in ways that most children (or adults) couldn't possibly imagine. At 11 years of age, Sundari was taken for three months' worth of training by the Liberation Tigers of Tamil Eelam, their war against the government having long included the use of child soldiers.

Maybe, for Sundari, it's better to make jokes, even after things like the tsunami, which sadly, pitifully, wasn't the worst thing she'd ever seen or had happen to her. The natural disaster, unlike the threat of war, went away and didn't come back; the ocean's waves didn't ask children to become suicide bombers for a cause.

"In big battles we shoot together
so we don't know whose bullet killed people."
– Former child soldier

Chapter 2
Soldier Girl

They didn't smile too much, the first children who came to call
Grace Care Center their home. Their emotions, understandably, ran
from anger to sadness, from loss of faith to, sometimes, fear of being
in line for additional punishment.

On August 31, 2002, Eric Parkinson, Rev. Jeyanesan and a small,
fledgling staff welcomed 10 girls to Grace Home, located not far from
the school they would attend, the Methodist Girls College (primary
school), in the heart of Trincomalee.

Ten different stories, with many things in common: The girls
were made orphans by war or poverty; most were from Sri Lanka's
northern regions, to include the Jaffna peninsula. They'd seen tragedy,
up close and personal, from the deaths of their fathers to the rapes or
suicides of their mothers. (Widows in the region, often stigmatized by
northern culture, were prone to self-administered death, with methods
including drinking poison or lighting themselves afire.)

Some of the first Grace girls were referrals from UNICEF, the
United Nation's children's advocacy organization, which rescued them
from training camps run by the Liberation Tigers of Tamil Eelam.
By then it was no secret in Sri Lanka that the Tigers – and other
paramilitary groups – were recruiting children to fight their war.

Most of the girls were sullen, fearful of the ongoing misery or
punishment that had made up so much of their lives. Among them,
however, was an outgoing presence quickly noticed by staff and visitors:

Sundari, a 12-year-old from the village of Killinochchi. Marked by emotional trauma unimagined in most of the world, Sundari had a particular spark to her personality, the promise of hope stubbornly maintained through life's harshest challenges.

Born in 1989, in a village barely maintaining a meager existence, Sundari's family was challenged further in 1999, when her father died a poor man's death from malaria. An active, intelligent, funny (and, yes, sometimes pouty) child, Sundari was cautious of her new surroundings when first told she would live at Grace. Relocations were a frequent childhood companion for these girls, with displacements from bombed-out villages, changes in school forced by the destruction of buildings, and a nomadic instinct to seek slightly greener pastures elsewhere on the small island.

There had been periods, frustratingly brief, of a stable life. Children always find a way to smile, and Sundari and her friends believed, sometimes, that they were lucky, when it seemed like the whole, entire village celebrated festivals. A favorite tradition was Pongal, a harvest-time tribute to thank God and the sun for the season's crops. Milk rice, among other precious treats, was boiled in hopes of spilling over on the east side of the clay pot, a harbinger of good fortune and better days to come.

With neighboring children, Sundari enjoyed occasional times that allowed for school and play, for net ball or hide-and-seek, or for gathering around a small table in the afternoon shade of a tree, pretending to enjoy a peaceful meal of rice and curry and a relaxed cup of tea. "Doll house," the children in Sri Lanka call it, a translated name for a universal game. When played in a Third World combat zone, the make-believe meals and dreams were of more than just playing grown-up; food was as precious a commodity as the hope for peace in for girls born into war.

**

Most official accounts report 1983 as the starting point of the Tamil-Singhalese war. Tamils call it "Black July," a bloody month that

Discouraging to both wildlife and those who view young girls as a commodity, security in southern Asia is supported with embedded shreds of broken glass. Animals – and humans – may try to scale the barrier in search of coconuts or, at times, safety. (Photo by Lynn Helland.)

began with the massacre of a Sri Lankan Army patrol by members of the LTTE. In response, Singhalese groups – some affiliated with the nation's security forces, others acting independently – killed an estimated 3,000 Tamils during a week's worth of rioting and property burning. Hardly an integrated nation before the war, the violence further segregated the population. Up to 100,000 Tamils living in and around Colombo fled north and east, just as Singhalese citizens of those regions began relocating in large numbers to the south and west.

Unofficially, the seeds of war were planted earlier. From a Tamil standpoint, the conflict started in June 1981, when one of history's largest book-burnings took place at the University of Jaffna, long considered one of southern Asia's cultural jewels. Sri Lankan security forces destroyed nearly 100,000 items in the institution's library and museum, including palm leaf-manuscripts dating back to before Buddha found enlightenment or Jesus Christ walked the earth, objects of art and literature that redefine the term "irreplaceable."

Before taking up arms, the Liberation Tigers of Tamil Eelam formed as a political organization, one of a host of groups claiming to represent a segment of the population in a still-young democracy. Numerous parties – with either Singhalese or Tamil interests – were formed after Ceylon shook off colonial rule. For Singhalese activists, it was a chance to properly balance the scales, which they felt erred too heavily with a minority that received disproportionate favoritism with government jobs and educational opportunities. (Access to the national payroll allowed for a better living for many Sri Lankans – the government controlled business ranging from banking to media to health care and more.)

Some believed it was time for the country's identity to be confirmed: The question of which of the two principal ethnic groups could lay claim to having first settled the island was as timeless as Sri Lanka itself. The division widened in the post-colonial era, sparked by political decisions including the 1956 Official Language Act, which declared Sinhalese to be the country's "one official language," followed by a Constitutional amendment in 1972 that mandated, "Buddhism shall have the foremost place" among religious beliefs.

At first, the opposition was mostly political. Groups including the Tamil United Liberation Front and others sought a proportionate Tamil voice in official matters. Parties came and went, each having little impact on policies and politics. Using the Tamil name "Eelam," meaning "homeland," the LTTE formed in 1976 as a youth-lead militant group that carried a more aggressive stance than previous organizations. Organized by Velupillai Prabhakaran, their goal was a separate homeland for Tamils, and they were determined to reach that goal.

The Tiger reputation grew over the years, notably as masters if not inventors of the suicide bomb attack; government tactics equally began raising international eyebrows, with the cautious phrase "ethnic cleansing" used to describe government activities.

With each passing year, the war grew more brutal in the number of incidents, escalated casualties and increasingly aggressive tactics. The Tamil population decreased from being 25 percent of the country's citizens in 1983 to barely 10 percent at the start of the 21st Century. By then, the population of Jaffna was half of its pre-war numbers, continuing a decades-long decline of Tamils. Living conditions and prospects in Sri Lanka shrank. The conflict all but halted the lucrative tourist industry that's a natural for a tropical paradise rimmed by beaches. The principal exports were losing their worth in the world market as reports of human rights abuses committed by both sides of the conflict mounted and international financial aid shrank.

Outside diplomacy was attempted, notably from India, a country once landlocked with Sri Lanka at the southern Tamil Nadu province; Indian involvement was partly motivated by a cautious eye toward any "independence" thoughts from that region, where an estimated 100,000 Sri Lankan Tamil exiles sought refuge by 1985.

The central and state governments of India supported, off and on, both sides of the conflict during its first decade. In 1987, India faced its own Tamil unrest, sparking fears among LTTE leaders of an invasion from the north. That same year, the Indian administration of Rajiv Gandhi, without consulting the rebel group, negotiated an agreement on their behalf with the government. The treaty was nevertheless signed, both by the LTTE and other Tamil resistance groups, and a monitoring body was created, the Indian Peace Keeping Force, which would move in to northern areas, disarm the Tigers and take over security from a Sri Lankan Army that would, under the agreement, retreat.

The pact, however, was not agreed to by all Sri Lankans, and Singhalese and Muslims rioted in the south, claiming that the government caved in to pressure from India, which they believed would soon occupy their country and, perhaps, return them to colonial status. The peace treaty dissolved, as others would over the years.

Subsequent negotiations, however, would need to consider additional interests in the conflict, as other political parties took up arms. A 1989 Singhalese rebellion in the south marked the first appearance of a political group with a Marxist agenda, the Janatha Vimukthi Peramura (JVP) party, the "People's Liberation Front," which launched a series of political murders. In response, government forces sent death squads out to murder JVP suspects, whose bodies littered the nation's rivers during a three-year reign of terror that, nationwide, resulted in at least 3,000 deaths.

The LTTE no longer trusted the governments of India or Sri Lanka; India briefly waged war against the LTTE before withdrawing in 1990, when a second agreed-upon ceasefire ended quicker than the first. The former Tiger ally Gandhi was assassinated in 1991 by a suicide bomber believed to be the work of the LTTE. (Denials were issued at first, although Prabhakaran later issued statements of regret over the killing.) Gandhi had resigned in 1989 after a general election defeat, but was determined to regain office.

The ground-based kamikaze attack became the Tiger's trademark, carried out by "Black Tiger" squads. A second political leader, Sri Lankan President Ranasinghe Premadasa, was killed by a suicide bomber in 1993, and in 1999, President Chandrika Bandaranaike Kumaratunga, two days before being elected to her second term, was targeted by an LTTE suicide bomb that left her without sight in one eye.

It was a brutal, complicated war, waged in part by armed groups determined to continue the fight in spite of a rapidly shrinking number of potential soldiers. What the International Red Cross called the "No Mercy" war escalated its recruitment of children over the years: Boys in uniform before their 16th birthday were common, and girls, in time, were subject to the same conscription.

In Killinochchi, Sundari no sooner recovered from the loss of her father when her family was told they remained obligated to send one member for training by the Tamil Tigers. Sundari was the only option, and at age 11 she was told that she might have to die for her people to have a future.

***

The Tigers maintain that children – girls – are not trained for military operations. They don't, said Steepan Thiyosan, a former Tiger living near Trincomalee, deny that participation by each family is mandatory. The sessions are voluntary, he said, and amount to little more than watching some video.

"They show films, give speeches, and let them know what the mission is about," Thiyosan said. "They do not take anyone by force. It's a free invitation. If they're willing to fight for the Tamils, they can join."

Although denying the combat training, Thiyosan explained the motivation held by the Tiger cadre and taught to the children: "The government is treating the Tamils like slaves," said Steven. "So the Tamils should support [the Tigers'] fight."

The struggling civilians of Sri Lanka's north and east had so many challenges to overcome; they were no longer outraged at the violence, or the brutality involving children. Sending children to war had been the norm for too long. "This is what life is," the girls are told, sadly by their parents, with armed determination by Tiger instructors. Their life would be filled with suffering, discrimination, and death, and they'd seen and known of too many incidents to disagree. Beginning in the early 1990s, reports of "round-ups" became increasingly frequent, with 100 or more Tamils taken into custody. (One example among dozens that were investigated was a September 1990 raid in Batticaloa, in which 181 people – including 35 children under the age of 10 – were taken and killed. Numerous mass graves would be discovered in the years ahead.)

When, exactly, the practice of child conscription began is unknown, and for years it remained local gossip. When international ears began hearing too many stories to dismiss, UNICEF investigations were allowed. The results were starling. In mid-2006, more than 1,500 underage fighters were reportedly wearing Tiger uniforms; an estimated 50 children a month were being recruited in the north and east.

For many girls in the Tiger camps, the motivations may have been even more personal. One former child soldier told a United Nations researcher of watching her father die: "They created an argument and dragged him out," she said of the visit to a humble home by armed troops. "They hit him, and shot him in the temple. The brain came out and he fell."

Children knew that torture that was rampant in northern Sri Lanka, of men being put in tar barrels and burned while trapped among smoldering tires, of babies being put into boiling water, of, "People in the border villages being cut up," one girl remembered.

Young girls talk, teenage girls talk a lot, and Sundari heard the stories from the child survivors, even before she lived them herself. Sundari was 10 when she lost her father; by then the war was approaching 20 years. When she went to Tiger training camp, it seemed at first to be just another displacement, another time of being taken somewhere (or having loved ones taken away). This time was different, though.

"It was difficult for me to live there," Sundari said. "I was scared at first, and did not know any of these people."

Training someone, even a child, to handle a weapon is not as difficult

A life spent in war: At the Rawatha orphanage (above) in Trincomalee, a small home managed by Buddhist monk Kamamaldeniye Pamgnabissa, the realities of war include a bunker, into which the children have many times fled when explosions from the nearby jungle get too close. During times of increased hostilities, Sri Lanka security forces (below) spend each morning scouring the roadsides for claymore mines that may have been set overnight.

as convincing scared little girls that they might have to kill others. The general theme of the speeches was, "Come join the LTTE to fight for our country." The unspoken message was that they had no choice.

"Listening to the lectures made me feel good about dying for my country," Sundari said. "I thought it was the right thing to do."

In a camp about 100 kilometers away from her home, Sundari spent nearly three months learning to fight as a soldier. The day started at sunrise, with duties and chores before breakfast. Mornings included running, karate, learning to handle claymore mines, compass reading and code sending, and courses in escape and evasion techniques suitable to many environments.

Also featured was weapons training, including AK-47s (capable of discharging 600 rounds per minute), and T-56 assault rifles. Smaller children and those unaccustomed to weapons were, at first, given "dummy" rifles, learning to become "one" with the gun before graduating to the real thing. The rifle was their constant companion, even while sleeping on the dirt floor of a shed shared with a dozen other children.

Afternoons and evenings included films and lectures. Physical fitness was taught to 10-year-old girls by having them do push-ups on their fists. Discipline included holding a rifle overhead while doing forced sit-stand repetitions, made all the more difficult as the girls were punched and kicked by grown men while performing the exercise.

It wasn't all just training. Willing or not, children were often used as soldiers and considered the same, by Tiger cadre and opposing security forces. The stories the girls heard were becoming more frequent, resulting in an increasing number of charges filed by humanitarian agencies that alleged the most brutal crimes imaginable. Government soldiers were accused of sexually abusing Tamil girls; in some cases, the gang rape of girls as young as five or six years old was reported.

That was Sundari's reality, told in whispered accounts; common knowledge in villages where a population had grown used to living in fear, and anger.

Some of the older girls in camp were issued the distinctive, Bengal-

At Grace Care Center, children with similar experiences to "Sundari" preferred, given an option, the pursuit of peace over the martyrdom of war. Some of the first residents of Grace were, before being recommended to the home, conscripted into training by armed groups. Dozens of children were able to finish their education and pursue a better opportunity for themselves.

striped Tiger uniforms. Matching fatigues, however, were not necessary to participate in the conflict. Pairs of girls as young as 10 were sent wearing simple dresses on missions to government checkpoints. When the guard looked at one girl's identification, the other moved to the rear for a clean, easy shot from a rifle they'd carried, hidden under their simple dresses.

Some were ordered to do more than kill others. The girls were told that it was a great honor to die a hero's death, after which they would be promoted to a higher rank and given a hero's status and funeral. The one item of jewelry the girls were given was a simple black thread, from which hung a vial holding a cyanide capsule. This, they were told, was to be taken if they were captured, where it was likely that they would be sexually abused by security forces.

One surviving child soldier told a United Nations researcher of the period she spent as a prisoner, held captive by Singhalese troops. Her experience, she said, rendered her incapable of ever being able to have a husband.

"There is no one who will understand me," she said, having been stigmatized from not only being a Tiger, but from having been raped, by men individually or by groups using objects including bottles to sexually penetrate a child. She described being hung by her feet and beaten while a cellophane bag was held over her head.

"I will never, ever marry a man," she said; no man "Could ever understand how miserable a human being, a girl, can be."

In spite of the justifications preached by the Tigers, the girls instinctively knew what they had done was wrong. One girl spoke of knowing that a Tiger raid on a village she participated in shouldn't have included shooting a baby. If they had to kill, she said, she preferred the more impersonal encounters: "We usually fight in the night, so you don't see how many you shoot," said one girl. "In big battles, we shoot together so we don't know whose bullet killed people."

Some believed they were branded for life as guerillas or traitors, insurgents or terrorists; labels too complicated for teenage girls to fully understand, but the resulting reputation wasn't lost on them.

"I don't think other people in this country will ever feel good toward us," one said. "The way I feel about my family and my people, they also feel about theirs. We lost that trust forever."

Every story has two sides, and on a personal, one-on-one level, some of the children reported encounters that offered a sliver of hope. One girl spoke of being treated kindly by an Army man, who found the small, frightened girl lying injured in the jungle, and took her to a hospital. It was a random act of kindness that may have convinced one person to commit one less act of aggression.

By that point in the conflict, however, too many people understood a fundamental truth about war learned by a girl barely into her teens:

"If I don't shoot to kill the enemy, I will be killed."

***

Some of the girls who would be soldiers managed to escape; many died in combat. Sundari was among the fortunate ones, spared from death and, in a rare opportunity, given a choice between war and peace.

Entering its second decade, the civil conflict's results were evident. When Grace Care Center first became Grace Home to 10 scared children, during the first legitimate series of peace talks in years, most accounts estimated that the war had produced 65,000 casualties. That figure was adjusted in the years to follow, with multiple discoveries of mass graves adding to the total number. A report by Rev. Jeyanesan in 2004 estimated 78,000 war casualties just among the Tamil population, 60,000 of whom were civilians. Rev. Jey claimed that Singhalese losses were estimated at 35,000, of which only 5,000 were civilians. (Southern Singhalese were less at risk: Although the Tigers have often carried out ambushes in Colombo, the principal theaters of war were in the north and east.) Although Jeyanesan's numbers inflated official estimates, the ratio of combatant to civilian was consistent with the reports given by international news agencies.

During that period of relative calm, other facts about the war were being calculated. A February 2002 United Nations Report was among the early documents urging governments and paramilitary organizations to curb the use of child soldiers – citing the practice in Angola, Colombia, the Philippines and, notably, Sri Lanka, which exceeded the age and gender limits of the other three nations.

In 2002, the Asia Pacific Center for Justice and Peace reported that, although the Sri Lankan government was party to the Geneva Convention rules of conflict and engagement, and the Tamil Tigers pledged adherence to the same policy, "Both sides are guilty of torture, illegal detention, disappearances and extra-judicial executions." Thousands of abductions were documented over the years. Amnesty International reported that more than 100 children a month were taken from their homes in government controlled areas, equal to the numbers attributed to the Tigers in the north. (In spite of growing awareness and concessions made by both sides, Amnesty International claimed that in mid-2006 more than 1,500 child soldiers were still wearing Tiger stripes.)

Restoring the hopes and faith of these children would be a challenge. One former child soldier told the United Nations she no longer enjoyed going to temple, and wanted to know: "Why did God allow this to happen to me?"

In that first summer at Grace Care Center, there was reason to believe that a future was possible. The cease-fire agreement appeared to be taking hold, and negotiations were taking place in Colombo. Each passing day of silence from the war teased Sri Lankans into believing another might follow. The children who came to Grace in August 2002 were not always smiling, and often afraid. They had plenty to be frightened of, but Sundari insists she was not scared, at least, not for herself. In an early indication of the leader she would become, she was concerned about the younger girls, those in her group and the littlest ones who take part in the day-care activities at Grace.

The children were scared, but Grace Home quickly became just that. Grace realized the dream of Parkinson, who wanted the children to feel a sense of belonging, of peace, of space. A garden playground was born on the property bearing the motto: "Where true peace allows children the freedom to be children." Parkinson wanted Sundari and her friends to dream of a life of peace and opportunity.

For Sundari, the lessons took hold.

"When I came to live at Grace Home, I didn't want to fight," Sundari said. "I can study and become a teacher."

In the years after Grace became home to 100 girls, the war returned, often, to Trinco, and Sundari did her best to keep the younger girls from being too afraid. When explosions were heard nearby, she entertained the staff and children with jokes and comedy, with imitations of the workers and ministers they all knew, to help take their minds off the conflict.

"The small children suffer from the noise," Sundari said of occasional explosions that, at times, could be heard every few days. "It makes me worried."

Beyond the walls of the Grace, Sundari saw the results of war. By the time she was old enough to be a leader to younger children, a role model for those who had few such inspirations, Sundari made her decision, a simple choice between war and peace:

"I don't want to be a Tiger anymore."

Stuffed Animals and Things That Explode

It had already been a long day when Hiram Labrooy said: "Don't step on the land mines."

"What?!" asked (shouted) the other American in our group, a college student bringing up the rear of a single-file march. He froze in his tracks, waiting for further information about potential explosives.

We were hiking through shrubs and shattered homes, a former fishing village on Sri Lanka's northeast coast. Labrooy, our guide and translator, casually pushed branches aside, crouched when necessary, and invited us to follow his lead.

Also, he advised: "Don't step on the land mines." Hesitating long enough for us to pause, and hold our breath, Labrooy smiled and pointed to various animal droppings on the ground. "Land mines," he laughed. "See?"

A real funny guy, Labrooy, our driver, friend and – for want of a better description – the "go-to" guy at Grace Care Center. Labrooy's humor covered a wide spectrum, from the dry and satiric to the silly and slapstick. The warning about explosives on the ground was of the subtle, low-key variety: Earlier that morning, we posed for photos next to a billboard that encouraged, "Ban land mines for safe future." Comedy is about timing, no matter the language, and the subject of explosives was never far from attention. Leftover ordinance lay scattered across the landscape, difficult to detect amid the ruins of disaster and war. The tsunami relief efforts of international volunteers shared space with Dutch mine-sweepers, who continued the work they had started years earlier: Delicate walks through uncharted fields to locate still-potent explosive devices, hoping to prevent further casualties of war. (I'd met some of those victims, including a 12-year-old whose left hand was blown off when, as a little boy, he played with a stray land mine.)

Hiram Labrooy, an idealist with a Holden Caulfield complex, embodies "Catcher in the Rye" dreams whether as unofficial "big brother" to the girls of Grace, or, as he grew with the orphanage, manager of Mercy Home.

We were a few dozen kilometers north of Trincomalee, in the company of two men who lost their homes to the tsunami. They now lived in an Internally Displaced Persons camp further inland, unable to rebuild on property they once owned. The government had declared a "buffer zone," in which it claimed possession of uninhabited land within a few hundred meters of the shore, for potential use when (and if) tourism could again boost the local economy. (International observers and diplomats, to include former United States Presidents George H.W. Bush and Bill Clinton, lobbied with limited success to have this policy modified.)

We spent much of the morning at the camp, meeting families who were trying to rebuild shattered lives. The sturdy shelters were small, but better than many other options: On the trip from Trinco we met a family of more than a dozen people who shared a small, roadside tent of patchwork construction. An invitation was extended to visit the village that many of the IDP families once called home, a small, close community now reduced to shattered brick that would soon disappear into the landscape.

"They want to go home, but they cannot," Labrooy shrugged. No jokes, no games played with mock innocence to fool a gullible visitor; his ability to laugh was inspired because – not in spite – of the tragedies he'd seen.

Labrooy made himself quickly known to the volunteers at Grace Care Center. In the months following the tsunami, when VeAhavta groups were a near-constant presence, Labrooy routinely worked 16, 17-hour days to make sure the guests were able to do everything possible on an endless checklist of projects. He possessed a range of natural skills well suited to a variety of opportunities, and served as coordinator, advisor, guide and translator, with solid, conversational English along with both Sinhala and Tamil fluency.

In turn, he learned (perhaps too much) about western culture from his growing circle of American friends. Not everything was internationally understood or available in tourist guidebooks, including certain colloquial gestures; informal "sign language" declarations such as Italian hand-salutes or the singular statement of an extended middle-finger. During another visit, we were in the van en route to Trinco, when I noticed on the floor a surgical glove that had been inflated and tied as a hand-shaped balloon. Someone (obviously one of our visiting team) pricked pinholes to deflate three of the glove's four fingers. The result was a blue fist poking a defiant middle digit.

"Nice," I smiled, trying to guess the likely culprit. (Given that particular group of travelers, there were several candidates.)

Labrooy didn't understand the glove's symbolism. I explained the gesture's meanings and implications. He chortled, giggled, and enthusiastically wedged the rubber hand under the windshield. We drove on with a rolling blue salute offered to the passing landscape: Three-wheel taxis; bicyclists bearing burdens strapped across the rear wheel-frame; security forces stationed at intersections. (Seeing which, I realized it was a good thing that some expressions are not universally understood. Flipping off the troops in a police state could be considered an unnecessary risk.)

It was interesting that, with Colombo sporting McDonald's and posters for the latest Brad Pitt-Angelina Jolie movie, some things crossed the planet while others didn't. We discussed the methods different cultures used to "tell someone off," or express street-level contempt; most cross-reference dictionaries don't include the definitions of middle fingers or thumbed noses. In south Asia, men looking to start a fight may hold their hands together in front of them, and split them in opposite directions, indicating someone who "goes both ways," a challenge to another man's masculinity.

The contemptuous window ornament went unnoticed by those it greeted, which was just as well. The challenge in an American barroom found in a juvenile gesture must have seemed trivial to Labrooy, as would comparable communications when cast in Sri Lanka. Compared to the threat of armed forces that represented a variety of interests, how serious was a meaningless insult compared to the daily task of staying alive.

In many ways, Labrooy was his own minority in a nation filled with marginalized populations. Of mixed heritage, he carried a variety of presentations suitable to circumstance, and put them to work as needed. He'd had opportunities to seek a better life elsewhere, and was better equipped than most to find safer pastures. At times a mysterious figure, the stories shared

Postcards from Trinco: Shortly before Hiram Labrooy joked about stepping on land mines, the author (left) and University of Michigan student Alex Papo (right) posed with Sri Lankan journalists at Trincomalee General Hospital, next to a banner advocating the elimination of explosive devices. (Below) Along the roadside north of Trincomalee, a family of nine lived in this makeshift tent after losing their fishing home to the tsunami.

by visitors with whom he became close were of a one-man contradiction of uncertain validity.

As with whispered accounts of atrocities committed against children, or the legends and lore of a country with ancient origins, the rumors about Labrooy couldn't all be true, but there were too many with common denominators to all be fiction.

Away from the orphanage, Labrooy lived in a simple, comfortable house he shared with – and provided for – his mother and brother. He gave us a tour of the modest, clean home, situated off a dirt path leading from Trinco, within echo distance of occasional explosions from the nearby jungle.

After showing us the sitting room and kitchen, he drew back a curtain to show us his bedroom. His quarters were on the small side: a single bed dominated the space, which included a cabinet for his clothes and a small table holding the usual assortment of photos, keys, colorful Sri Lankan currency and a CD by the reggae-influenced group, UB40.

"Oh, for God's sake," I looked at Labrooy.

"What?" He smiled, knowing that I was joking, teasing him.

On his bed were several fluffy, stuffed animals. Not many American guys, I told him, were comfortable enough with themselves to A) Possess stuffed animals; or B) allow other people to know it.

"These are my friends" he smiled again, giggled, and picked up one of the toys and gave it a hug.

The walking contradiction of Labrooy matched the dual nature of Sri Lanka itself. He seemed innocent, at times, with child-like qualities and a playful personality; the toys were an indulgence away from the realties surrounding his home. He was also a lean, muscular young man with savage kick-boxing skills who survived a life surrounded by brutal violence. An idealist with a Holden Caulfield complex, Labrooy embodied "Catcher in the Rye" dreams as he played unofficial big brother to the orphan girls of Grace Care Center. He treasured the innocence of the children, the serenity of Grace, with a ferocious intensity. He was all-too familiar with the dangers of letting the children fall over the cliff.

Sometimes, people stepped on landmines if they weren't careful.

*"In the deeps of the jungle
and the remoteness of the mountains
were the ruined cities and moldering temples,
mysterious relics of a forgotten time and vanished race."*
– Mark Twain, "Following the Equator: A Journey Around the World."

Chapter 3
A Miracle at Third Milepost

By early afternoon, the people were suffering in the blazing heat. Even by near-equatorial standards (Sri Lanka is parked less than 15 degrees north of the planet's center ring), temperatures of 110-degrees Fahrenheit tested the thousands of souls who gathered at the gates of Grace Care Center.

Most of those in the crowd, Rev. S. Jeyanesan knew, were ailing even before the heat added to their misery. They'd come to Grace seeking free medical attention, and formed lines at the entrance well before sunrise. By the afternoon, tempers flared, at times, among those desperate to get some help for families, wives, and children.

When the sun was at its most severe, Rev. Jey told an American minister he would pray for rain, and went inside the modest chapel to ask for divine assistance. Not long after Jeyanesan said "amen," the minister told people back home (and swore it was true), clouds formed and cooling rains fell from the sky.

It may not have happened exactly that way: Different reports were offered from others who were there, in which hours – not minutes – separated the plea from the rain. Things happen at Grace Care Center, and culture-shocked, travel-numbed visitors may have told the occasional exaggeration.

It was a busy, confusing campus in even the quietest of moments, of which there were few during a 10-day clinic held in late 2003.

Thousands of patients sought help from "American doctors," as advertised on hand-made banners strung along Sri Lanka's east coast, from Trincomalee down towards Batticaloa. In the year since Grace Care Center opened, VeAhavta's volunteer base drew increasingly from the medical communities of southern California and Ann Arbor, Michigan, which sent teams of doctors on two-week missions to Trinco. Putting their skills to work on a grander scale was a natural extension of their involvement.

Among the volunteers who worked the clinic was Justin Yax, a 26-year-old intern from Michigan. Yax recalled taking an early-morning peek outside the front gate just hours before the operation began. The silence in the air, gently accented by the wash of the surf, was in sharp contrast to what awaited outside.

"The sun was just coming up," said Yax. On the access road, he saw the makings of a medical marathon that would join local stories about the growing orphanage: The crowd was beyond his wildest expectations.

"It was probably 50 people wide, and I couldn't see the end of it," Yax recalled. "That was what we had to look forward to."

Photographs, as with tales of rainmaking ministers, offered other perspectives. The road was wide enough for rows of 15, maybe 20 prospective patients.

The depth that Yax recalled, however, was accurate: By mid-morning, the line extended to the end of the access road, perhaps a quarter mile from the gate, and continued for more than a mile down the main road. "American Doctors at Third Milepost," the clinic was announced, which was all that was needed to bring masses of patients to the simple address in Uppuvelli, a crossroads three miles from the heart of Trinco. "Grace Church" was becoming shorthand in the community for a place where help could be found.

From Sept. 29 through Oct. 12, 2003, "Mercy Clinic" gave some of Sri Lanka's most destitute citizen's access to free health care. The patient load greatly exceeded the predictions of the crew, which

In spite of the availability of 21st Century technology in some places, transportation in villages surrounding Trincomalee sometimes dates back to a far earlier time. Observers noticed that many families in struggling communities were better equipped to survive the tsunami's aftermath than those who had adapted to modern, urban survival in Colombo or other southern cities.

included 23 doctors along with nurses, physician's assistants and other, non-medical volunteers.

The turnout, said Eric Parkinson, reflected the perceived status of visitors from the well-to-do west as seen by struggling survivors in developing nations.

"The banners were around, with a couple of buzz words on them," Parkinson said. "'American doctors' generated a lot of interest for whatever reason: Hard-trained doctors from the richest country in the world, they'll have the latest medicine, new techniques."

Sadly, for some of the patients who had great hopes but little understanding of medical limitations, there was no miracle cure waiting at the orphanage. Doctors did what they could for those with ailments that, sometimes, couldn't be addressed, regardless of the circumstance.

"Most of the people had these conditions that a one-time visit wasn't going to resolve," Parkinson said. "I know that was really frustrating to the doctors."

The results of war and poverty were widely on display, both in Trinco and along the nation's northeast coast. Yax, who arrived a few days ahead of the clinic's opening, accepted an invitation from Rev. Jey to visit Batticaloa while waiting for the rest of the team. Along the way – a route that required more than a few clearances at checkpoints maintained, depending upon the vicinity, by one side of the conflict or the other – Jey stopped as if struck by divine inspiration.

"We will have a clinic," Jey announced, and Yax scrambled to pull whatever tricks were possible from a basic medical bag for treatment that the most well equipped hospital could barely address.

"There was this kid, probably 14, with his little brother, who had muscular dystrophy," Yax said. "Very incapacitated, had a difficult time walking. His brother wanted me to do something about it. There's nothing you can do. If the kid were in America we could get devices, or social support; things that are available in other countries that aren't going to happen in a war-torn society."

Planned or improvised medical clinics were just part of the potential that the Grace Care Center demonstrated heading into its second year.

How legends are born: Learning that "American Doctors" were at Grace Care Center, patients waited outside the gate (above) in lines that formed up to the main road and well on the way to Trinco proper. (Photo courtesy Eric Parkinson) Access roads to town (below) are populated by pedestrians, cows, scooters, three-wheel taxis and bicycles, only occasionally interrupted by larger vehicles.

The girls' home was at capacity with 100 children in residence, and in the same month the clinic was held a Vocational Training Center opened to teach basic carpentry and computer classes (courses that, a year later, expanded to include sewing, welding, masonry and bicycle repair). The day care program launched in 2002 for indigent local children now provided more than 60 toddlers with a daily meal and basic pre-school lessons. In America, interest in VeAhavta and support for its plans grew, and so did potential plans for the compound.

The realization of those plans, however, rested on the delicate hopes that the still-fresh cease-fire would lead to a chance for the region to rebound from battle-scarred poverty. In spite of the previous year's truce between the Government of Sri Lanka and the Tamil Tigers, the clinic was held in an atmosphere more cautious than hopeful.

***

Between Trinco and Batticaloa are patches of territory controlled by the LTTE, landscape that includes a cemetery for fallen Tigers buried with honors – "Arlington style" – Parkinson described the symmetrical rows of markers. It was one of many, on both sides: In the early days of the ceasefire, graveyards both military and civilian bore many acres of freshly turned earth. Tamilnet, the Tiger-sympathetic online news service, reported claims of mass graves discovered in the northern region Chemmani, said to hold the bodies of some of the 600 Tamils who "disappeared" during the conflict: Thousands of relatives and loved ones finally learned the fatal truth after years of uncertainty.

Two decades of war and poverty extract other casualties, byproducts of the conflict and ethnic violence. In the early 21st century, Sri Lanka continued to hold one of the world's highest rates of suicide, with a self-inflicted death reported every 40 seconds. Most disturbing to researchers was the average age of the suicides: In the 1950s, Sri Lankan elders were at the highest probability of suicide; by the 1970s, men and women age 15 to 30 ranked highest among suicide age groups. During the 1980s and into the next century, that average age was even lower, as children began taking their own lives in increasing numbers.

Prospects for peace, as far as the public belief in the process, became mired between truth and rumor, fact and legend. When the LTTE temporarily withdrew from the negotiations in 2003 – demanding more definitive proposals for a political solution – the drafts and counter-drafts were, to the ears of many Sri Lankans, just more talk from "the politicians" and the Tigers. Both sides had issues to resolve: In Colombo, President Chandrika Bandaranaike Kumaratunga rejected an early proposal from the LTTE. Peace talks were still on hold when, in 2004, Kumaratunga dissolved the parliament and called for an election, the results of which elevated the authority of her political party, the United People's Freedom Alliance.

The news from Jaffna was equally confusing: The latest twist in a complicated rebel structure was added that year when LTTE officer Vinayagamoorthi Muralitharan, going under the title "Colonel Karuna," formed a breakaway faction of the Tigers, one not interested in negotiating with the government. Some questioned the legitimacy of Karuna's Tiger stripes, and whispers were heard that the government might have facilitated his rise to power (to include aiding the Colonel's escape during a brief skirmish Karuna launched just south of Trincomalee).

Throughout Sri Lanka, it was difficult to know what to believe. The state-owned print and broadcast media often seemed to be just another political tool, if not part of the conflict. Along with suicide rates, the number of slain reporters in Sri Lanka was among the highest in the world. Tamil-sympathetic reporter Aiyathurai Nadesan, a correspondent in Batticaloa, was killed in broad daylight on May 31, 2004, one of more than a dozen journalists who would be struck down just in the years since the cease-fire.

Reports were as conflicting as folklore, telling the same stories with individual adjustments or exaggerations. In this environment, the clinic held at Grace Care Center – told by the thousands of patients who filed through the gates – joined the growing awareness of this new facility that mixed fact with hearsay.

Children enrolled in the day care program, including (from left) Vijaya Kamoolan, Kuthubdeen Ameerken and Uthaya Kumar, were able to see American doctors when VeAhavta volunteers were in town. Opportunities for medical clinics along Sri Lanka's east coast included countless improvised villages (below) that line the road between Trinco and Batticaloa.

Stories were also told by the visitors themselves, their senses reeling from the overpowering sights, sounds and experiences that began with a 48-hour door-to-door trip to one of the most beaten, suffering regions on earth. Yax spent his first two days at Grace Care Center as the lone visitor while awaiting the crew from California, and was amazed at the atmosphere from the moment he entered the orphanage, a place he'd heard so much about, seen pictures of but couldn't accurately imagine.

"It was just ... amazing, beautiful," Yax said. "There was a solitary porch light on, and all these girls sitting there, waiting for me."

From there it was a whirlwind. While waiting for the clinic to start, Yax traveled to Batticaloa, conducted mini-clinics at refugee camps or – following the inspiration of Rev. Jey – on the spur of the road-side moment in places he remembered as, "Hell and gone from nowhere."

Away from the population centers of Batticaloa or Trinco, miles upon miles of barren field, jungle edge or semi-wetlands passed by without human interruption. Those who needed medical attention, even had they owned a bicycle, wouldn't have been up to the day-long (or more) pedal to the nearest village.

Parkinson recalled one woman, "Whose job was to smash rocks into smaller rocks, making gravel for roadways. That's what she did, hour after hour; no safety equipment, just a hammer," Parkinson said. "One of these rocks shattered, and a good-size shard of granite was in her eye."

They transported the woman to Batticaloa Hospital, where the shard was successfully removed. It was one injury among many, with patient needs from every chapter and section of a medical textbook. Many in those regions, Yax said, drank from rain ditches, suffered from respiratory illnesses or had infections approaching dangerous levels.

"This one kid had newspaper stuffed in his ear, to keep the pus from dripping on his shoulder," Yax said. "It was the worst case of outer ear infection: His ear drum was real red, tender, and if it goes to the inner ear, it could cause meningitis and the kid's dead."

The boy needed certain antibiotics that Yax did not have on hand. On the return trip, Yax and Rev. Jey revisited the improvised community, and delivered medicines obtained in Batticaloa to the patient who, as far as Yax could determine, survived yet another challenge of life in Sri Lanka.

Improvised clinics offered an intimate, personal connection with patients (the type, Yax said, that made most doctors study medicine in the first place), but the clinic at Grace was a non-stop blur of treatment. More than 23,000 patients were seen during days that started at a triage section staged on the children's playground before additional treatment was offered at improvised stations, with patients in the main hall, under tents in the yard or seated beneath a shade-providing tree.

Some said there were miracles at work that day. Astonishing tales were told, of inflated patient numbers or treatment outcomes, or of Rev. Jey's plea for rain that was answered within minutes. To both the visitors and the community outside its gates, Grace was increasingly able to inspire stories that took on mythical qualities. The sense of wonder held by the children of Grace and their neighbors about the visitors was matched by the esteem held by the Americans for the Sri Lankan friends they made.

Among those who came to Grace – not as a prospective patient but to offer volunteer service – was a 23-year-old translator. Hiram Labrooy first offered his services to Grace Care Center during the 10-day clinic, and would remain a key member of the compound for years.

***

Survival in Sri Lanka's northeast, Rev. Jey explained to Eric Parkinson, was a matter of adapting to one's environment.

"Jeyanesan used to joke, 'Always have your suitcase packed, and always be ready to swear your allegiance to whoever's in control,'" Parkinson said. "You've got to play to whatever audience is in front of you, and Hiram's learned to do that very well."

Hiram Labrooy came equipped with the right tools at the right time for Grace Care Center, the same skills that ensured his basic survival. Born in 1980 in a village near Trinco, by his early adult years Labrooy was responsible for his mother and at least one of his seven brothers and sisters at various times. To stay alive in northeast Sri Lanka, a young man came to terms with harsh, adult realities sooner than most would prefer. Survival, and safety, depended only partly upon being able to think for and defend yourself: Those abilities were considerable in Labrooy, who had some formal education to his credit along with military and martial arts training.

More important, however, was to know that allegiances in northern Sri Lanka shifted often with the conflict-driven winds; be prepared to agree with whoever knocked on your door, as Jey might advise. "Street smarts," an urban descendant of cultural folklore, was more essential than classroom lessons or the ability to fight.

"You have to take care of your life and your family," Parkinson said. "It's like dealing with a gang: It's not just you; they may come after your brother, your mom ..."

For survival's sake, Parkinson said, the melting-pot population of Trincomalee learned to become, in a word, political: Move among all different people, speak the language, do the dance. Labrooy was considered handsome – with lighter-than-average skin seen as having greater appeal – and worked on occasion as a male model. Shortly before he entered Grace Care Center for the first time, he was offered a small part in an independent film. (The rest of Labrooy's reported work history, as with many aspects of his personality, ranged from the practical to the unbelievable.) Acting would have come natural to Labrooy, who Parkinson watched in a variety of circumstances, playing before audiences of different backgrounds.

"I've seen him around Buddhist priests, and he does the traditional kissing of the feet," Parkinson said. "When he's around an Imam, or a Christian minister, he'll say what they want to hear. He's able to maneuver pretty well."

Labrooy well represented the inner conflict found in the Sri Lankan soul: Anger and violence pulling on one side; patience and peace on the other. Familiar with both, Labrooy described what might be called a drunken epiphany near a Buddhist temple, a late night's recognition of the destructive path his life was taking. Admittedly, he was looking for answers, afraid of what he might do if they went unfound.

In September 2003, Labrooy sensed an opportunity to apply some of what he wanted to do for the community he called – by choice – home. He volunteered service as a translator, met the volunteers (including "Mr. Justin Yax from Michigan") and quickly proved indispensable. Labrooy worked tirelessly throughout the clinic, often as the only person able to provide the necessary communications between doctor and patient, and spent 14-hour days running from station to station.

Following the clinic, VeAhavta doctors, including Michigan Dr. Naresh Gunaratnam and California Dr. Rushdi Cader, launched plans to put the medical clinic on the road, circling Grace Care Center in a wide arc to make regular visits to remote villages and Internally Displaced Persons camps. Making the project work required a local contact, skilled with an in-depth knowledge of the unmapped communities of forgotten civilians, and having enough formal education to work with medical equipment in a non-native language.

"Dr. Naresh told me about this program, that they needed a coordinator," said Labrooy. "I do not know anything about medicine, but he said, 'We think you can.'"

The American doctors taught Labrooy the rudimentary facts needed to get started, and he soon guided the rolling hospital to villages including Kinniya, a town south of the bay that suffered even more severe poverty than Trincomalee.

It wasn't all perfection at first. Spirited, energetic doctors put a tremendous amount of information before the young man.

"I was still very confused," Labrooy said. One destination failed when he, "Missed the bus station." Other communications broke down somewhere between dialects.

"I couldn't do the job very well," Labrooy said. "But Dr. Rushdi and Naresh, they told me what to learn."

Labrooy pledged to develop the necessary skills, on-the-job, within a month, and fulfilled that promise. He demonstrated a knack for

Among the youngest Grace girls in early 2008, Ramesh Dachayani, 8, smiles at "big sister" Subashini de Silva, 12, during a quiet afternoon in the Children's Park. (Photo by Hiram Labrooy) The younger children of Grace are assigned to "groups" headed by an older girl, providing a familial relationship and environment.

organization and the procurement of medicine, and the clinic began seeing an average of 80 patients per trip into the northeast's most remote communities. Patients were patients regardless of heritage, and Hiram moved with ease through Tamil or Singhalese populations, among worshippers of various faiths. That ability, as much as any other, made Labrooy the ideal candidate to help make Grace Care Center work.

As the orphanage grew to its capacity, the original vision was joined by consideration of other goals. Labrooy became resident jack-of-all-trades when VeAhavta visitors were at the compound. Either as a result of his street-smart instincts or his spiritual proclamations – either of which makes for good stories – Labrooy blurred the line between who was working for whom when volunteers were in town.

"If I do not make the maximum use of them, who is unfortunate?" Labrooy asked. "If you want to have a nice glass of lime juice, you must squeeze the lime as hard as you can to get a lot of juice. I need to serve the people, but I can't; I'm a poor man. They have a way to help the poor, and it doesn't matter if I get tired or exhausted."

Stories circulated of Labrooy coming to the rescue of both visitors and Grace's growing residency. When every shop was closed in Trinco during a security clamp down, the scooter-riding Labrooy left the safety of the orphanage and returned hours later with bags of rice to feed the children for another day or two. He found things when needed, made arrangements that seemed impossible, and was rarely stumped when a unique solution was needed to a problem. The tales, at times, stretched credibility, but the reality often matched the claim.

Although not a formal devotee of Siddhartha's teachings – in spite of the location of his life-purpose vision – Labrooy used Buddha-worthy examples to explain how to help others: "I saw a bird's nest at Grace, and watched one of the birds going out and collecting seeds to try to feed the other birds. It's a family; it's a good example. Nature teaches us so many things, we must watch those and try and add it in our lives."

Another story told of a day when Labrooy found a hand grenade – still capable of fulfilling its design – not far from a nearby schoolyard.

He took it to a hillside, and buried it deep so it would not kill anyone, let alone a child.

A noble thought, with a touch of Buddhist simplicity guiding its intention. Some might call it naïve, one grenade being a drop in the bucket of a country filled with explosives and a seemingly inexhaustible supply of those willing to use them.

On the other hand, Labrooy has also buried friends who were killed by grenades; and guns, and claymore mines. Those were memories he knew to be truth, not legend.

***

Parkinson has heard the stories, told by Grace staff, the children, the visitors: Tales of miraculous rain-making; some interesting anecdotes about Labrooy; or the one about the rows of trees planted on the eastern side of the compound, layers of thick evergreens sown between the beach and the children's dormitory rooms.

Several visitors, including Justin Yax, remember the explanation given by Rev. Jeyanesan for planting those trees.

"It's such a beautiful view," Yax reminded Jeyanesan. Why cover up a postcard-worthy look at the Indian Ocean?

Because, Jey reportedly told Yax, "God told me to."

"I said, 'Sure, you don't want to go against the Big Guy, right?'" Yax shrugged off the thought.

According to Parkinson, the trees were part of the plan from the beginning, to serve as a wind buffer to calm the often-harsh breezes coming off the ocean. It's one story, among many, that Parkinson said should be taken with a grain of salt. There's a fish-and-loaves quality to the tales, able to amaze or raise skepticism.

"It depends on who you were and how you were listening," Parkinson shrugged. "It's what people remember, or it's what they want to tell people."

Legends often have truth as a seed. A modest amount of fish and loaves did, in fact, feed those who were hungry on a long-ago Biblical day; at Grace, crowds of sweltering people did, in fact, survive the heat (with a little help from some afternoon rain that was a near-daily occurrence during monsoon season); and more than 23,000 souls were able to see a doctor they otherwise couldn't have.

Those beachfront trees, no matter the reason for being placed in the ground at Grace Care Center in early 2003, were in full bloom when the December 26, 2004 tsunami hit; rows of thick branches helped protect the children and buildings from the worst of the blast. The ocean's waves laid waste to the surrounding properties, while Grace survived mostly intact.

Encounters

Damage Tours and Burning Tires

It was an interesting time to discover that my companion, a Sri Lankan native, didn't speak a word of Tamil, Sinhalese or anything else our driver could understand.

One could also assume that the growing number of soldiers in the area didn't speak English, either.

"So you really don't know any of the language, huh?" I asked Naresh Gunaratnam, born in what was then called Ceylon but raised in England and the United States. He shrugged, and smiled, although he seemed equally concerned about our situation: Would the civil protests prevent our group from getting to Colombo for our scheduled flight home?

The immediate concern, stuck in a traffic gridlock at a barricade now swarming with soldiers, was if we could get back to the orphanage. We'd been gone from Grace Care Center since early morning, when I accepted Gunaratnam's invitation to what he called a "damage tour." My assumption was that he meant areas hit hardest by the disaster just a few weeks earlier, wreckage even more devastating than what we'd already seen.

Not quite. As the only one of our group who had been to Grace prior to the tsunami, Gunaratnam wanted to show me the problems that plagued the region long before the brutal waves came to shore – damage that would last longer and take far more effort to repair. The tsunami simply added to the already tragic number of orphans in the northeast. Rev. Jeyanesan reported at least another 100 boys lost their families to the disaster, just in the Trincomalee region.

Gunaratnam, an intense, driven doctor, and VeAhavta had made an impressive number of contacts in Trinco, a reputation that began well before the disaster, based in part on the medical missions and clinics at Grace.

To the glory of god
JDCSI
"GRACE CHURCH CARE CENTRE"
WAS
DECLARED OPEN
BY
MR. ERIC PARKINSON
(CHAIRMAN- VEAHAYTA, U.S.A.)
AND
DEDICATED BY
RT.REV.DR.S.JEBANESAN
(BISHOP IN JAFFNA)

ON 31ˢᵗ AUGUST 2003

By the time of the tsunami Grace Care Center had reached its capacity
of 100 children, launched day care and vocational training programs,
and seemed poised to expand beyond its modest walls. Grace was largely
spared from the tsunami's deadliest impact, but opportunities to extend its
assistance to others in the community rose after the disaster..

Among those was Dr. Ganhika Bahu, administrator of a small hospital clinic, who was highly regarded by local medical and school officials.

Bahu arranged an ambitious morning's agenda for us, provided a van and driver, and sent Gunaratnam and I to several facilities that were trying to make room for tsunami-affected children.

Orphanages from Batticaloa to Trincomalee were at – often beyond – capacity, housing the victims of war not found in battlefield casualty reports. A girl named Ithaya's father was shot while herding a cow back to pasture; her friend, Mayourini, watched her father taken from their home years earlier, and he hadn't been seen since. Both of these men were civilians. There were many stories, similar yet unique to the narrator; reports from little witnesses to a mother's suicide, a father's death.

The schools and children's homes struggled to meet the basic needs of the region's young. At one facility, a kitchen to feed 100 children amounted to one determined woman spending her days bent over a boiling pot, fueled by an open fire near a dusty courtyard. Food rations didn't increase with added children; each just received a little less.

After the final orphanage, we headed back to Bahu's clinic. Our driver turned onto a busy street in the market district, and came to an abrupt halt. A broken boat – of which Trinco's shores held a plentiful supply – had been dragged onto the roadway to block traffic. A makeshift barricade was being built from whatever materials were handy.

One street over, we ran into the same situation. A "hartal" was forming; the closing of roads and disruption of traffic and commerce enforced either by government barricades or through improvised, civilian-made roadblocks.

(We would hear several stories as to the inspiration for this particular hartal, either due to a political group's "claiming" of property near the fish market, or over what some considered an unfair percentages of relief supplies making their way to the east.)

Our driver was alert, and familiar with the winding streets of Trinco. Driving slightly ahead of the growing number of barricades, we made it back to the clinic. We asked Bahu about our prospects for getting to Grace.

Not to worry, the calm doctor said; the protest was more peaceful than

Shelter for the children: Orphanages in Trincomalee, including Sri
Shunmuga (above), struggled to meet the basic needs of children made
orphans by war and poverty. (Below) The tsunami of Dec. 26, 2004
left thousands of additional children without a home or family. Grace
Care Center was among the facilities trying to find room for the added
population of displaced families and orphan children.

aggressive. Hartals were frequent occurrences, matter-of-fact interruptions that were accepted as another byproduct of conflict and tensions. We would be safe, and our driver could get us through the disturbance.

We were relieved, and invited Bahu to join us for a late lunch.

"No," he sighed, "I must stay. There will be casualties." By his definition, this routine disturbance – and expected casualties – was not a major concern. Just another lousy day in paradise.

The hartal spread quickly to the outskirts of Trinco. Dozens of barriers formed on the harbor road: Long branches stacked in piles; a section of fence; ropes tied to utility poles at each side of the street. The obstructions were often enforced with burning tires, an addition both discouraging and theatrical.

Before long, the main roads were no longer passable. At a final barricade, dozens of grid-locked vehicles – vans, tuks, ox-carts, bicycles and anything else that rolled – intensified the emotions of both villagers and the security forces, now arriving at a steady rate. Soldiers rode to the scene two to a motorcycle, with the rear rider facing backward, rifle held at port arms.

At this definitive roadblock, the crowd pushed closer to a confrontation with the troops. Gunaratnam and I hoped to find a way past the barricade and complete the journey, if necessary, on foot. While we considered our options, a plastic water bottle flew from the crowd, aimed in the general direction of arriving troops; a moment that could have taken many turns. The bottle seemed to slow during its flight, allowing time to consider possible outcomes that could elevate the protest to a full-fledged riot.

In reality, time went rapidly, and activity remained relatively safe. There was some pushing, some shouting, confusion of rising volume. From the crowd, a pair of familiar faces greeted us: A tuk-tuk driver who on several occasions had driven me to Trinco; and Kunam, a resident of the camp next to Grace Care Center that was home to dozens of displaced families.

With little or no spoken communications (having discovered that Gunaratnam didn't speak the local language), Kunam understood our purpose, and joined us inside the van. He gave instructions to the driver, and we slowly turned around and drove away from the barrier, headed for a path leading to the rear entrance of Grace. Off the main road, the *hartal faded into the background as we drove a dusty trail that baked in the afternoon heat. Stray, undisturbed dogs found patches of shade that would remain in place until nightfall; a woman kept her young children inside while she prepared careful rations for the evening meal, knowing it might be days before more food would be available.*

Members of our sizeable group, more than a dozen, filtered back to the orphanage from wherever the morning's agendas had taken them. Stories were shared while plans were hatched. The decision was to leave that evening, rather than the following morning, taking advantage of a security-authorized window of opportunity before the next day, during which we were told the government's responding hartal would prohibit all travel.

It wasn't the good-bye we hoped for; the girls of Grace had rehearsed for days to present a talent show that evening, songs and dances and poems dedicated to a better future. Instead, nearly 100 girls sat cross-legged and crying in the main hall, sneaking glances at their new friends in the false hopes that that not everyone was leaving.

Dusk had fallen by the time we left Grace, a silent drive through Trinco and its surrounding villages, rolling slowly around barricades that glowed brightly with blazing tires. Roadblocks gave way to jungle paths through the highlands; lumbering elephants plodded through their nocturnal activities, at times crossing the road with little worry or concern.

In the morning, we enjoyed a leisurely breakfast at a guest house in Kandy, a resort town about 180 kilometers southwest of Trinco. The peaceful city included among its universities and attractions the Temple of the Tooth, a Buddhist monument predating the birth of Jesus Christ. There were no soldiers, no signs of the tsunami, no burning-tire barricades, and no children waiting for an audience to watch them sing, dance or pray for peace.

The hartal that prompted our early departure was, reports determined, inspired by a Singhalese activist group's taking of Tamil-owned property in Trincomalee. Within a few months, a statue would be placed on that ground, surrounded by soldiers and barbed wire, which many observers believe lead to the nation's return to war.

War and peace: On the final day in Trinco for a group of volunteers in February, 2005, a protest erupted after a Singhalese political group claimed Tamil-owned property. Road blocks (above) sprung up throughout the district as tensions elevated. The visitors made a hasty departure, and awoke the next morning in Kandy (below), just a few hours' drive yet so far removed from the struggles on the east coast.

"Then I stood on the sand ...
and I saw a beast rising up out of the sea."
– Revelation, Chapter 13

"They brought to Manu water for washing,
A fish came into his hands. It spake to him the word,
'A flood will carry away all these creatures'"
– Shatapatha-Brahmana (Story of Manu)

"By awakening, by awareness, by restraint and control,
the wise may make for oneself
an island which no flood can overwhelm."
– Wisdom of the Buddha (by F. Max Miller)

Chapter 4
Tsunami

At first, Hiram Labrooy dismissed the stories he heard as he cycled downtown to e-mail his sister before heading for work at Grace Care Center.

"The water is coming! Don't go there," people yelled.

So what, Labrooy thought, perhaps a pipe burst someplace, or the tide left an inland pool that covered the road. "I am not a piece of salt to dissolve," he told his friends, and continued toward the market district. Labrooy was irritated that people would try to cause panic; he was more concerned that it might be another, "Ethnic problem of war." He dismissed the stories of water, and told people not to spread false rumors.

"I scolded them in some bad language, and kept on going to town," he said.

A few minutes later, the ethnic problem was the furthest thing from Labrooy's mind. The ocean had, he saw, left its mark on Trincomalee,

Lest they forget: December 26, 2004 will long be remembered in Sri Lankan history and legend. This piece of driftwood was among the items thrown around the orphanage that morning; a fishing boat engine was found in the Children's Park, having been carried by the waves that roared past the shore more than 100 meters away.

leaving roads flooded more than a mile from the shore. As he carefully approached the coastline, with damaged buildings becoming unrecognizable ruins, he realized the problem was beyond his most fantastic imagination.

Early morning on Tuesday, December 26, 2004, an undersea earthquake sent tsunami waves roaring toward the Indian Ocean's many coasts. There were, in reality, two enormous waves. The first was deceptive of the disaster's strength, as it slowly, steadily swelled the ocean and quickly flooded villages and beaches.

The ocean retreated, further back than even the lowest tide levels, as if inhaling, long and deep, gathering strength before unleashing unprecedented power. The harbor emptied, briefly, leaving in its wake a muddy bed alive with flopping fish and anchored vessels. All along the lengthy coast, thousands of villagers ran onto the soggy floor to gather a bounty of food that would rival the best day's catch.

Then the real blast came, generated from the earthquake that rumbled off the northeast coast of Sumatra Island. The rush of water hit fast, all but extinguishing parts of Indonesia's Aceh Bandeh peninsula and pulverizing coastal towns in India, Thailand and Sri Lanka. The second wave crashed ashore at speeds measured in hundreds of miles per hour; waves of up to 40 feet or higher pounded whatever stood in their way, tearing through buildings without pause or mercy.

Labrooy was far enough away from the beach to avoid tragedy. He quickly turned his scooter toward Grace Care Center. The roads were crowded with people in search of help, or relatives. Labrooy focused on his destination, trying not to think of what he would find.

Approaching the Grace entrance, Labrooy first saw the ruins of the neighboring property; the Alles Gardens camp of displaced families might as well never have existed: Tents, lean-tos and the wood-stick huts of a small community were gone, replaced by swept-over sand and brush, upended trees and shattered fishing boats. The few possessions held by the residents were tossed further inland, or taken back out to sea.

At Grace, the brick wall supporting the gate – about 200 meters

Repairing and healing: In fishing villages along the coast (above), thousands of homes suffered damage that left most uninhabitable. The Government of Sri Lanka enacted a "buffer zone" that allowed authorities to claim abandoned properties as an investment for the anticipated, post-war tourist trade. (Below) Michigan doctors (from left) Gina Amalfitano, Naresh Gunaratnam and Bonnie Sowa toured Trincomalee General Hospital in February 2005 with attending physician Sathaharan Sundaralingam. "Dr. Satha" became a stable, constant friend to Grace Care Center.

from the shore – was shattered. Labrooy hurried inside, desperate to find his friends, the staff, the children.

Something resembling a miracle greeted Labrooy. After determining that all the children were safe, Labrooy toured the grounds for damage, and found less than he feared. The yard between the dormitories and the beach was littered with fallen trees (planted either due to divine inspiration or as a shield to oceanic winds), which had absorbed enough of the impact to spare the buildings from substantial damage. Neighboring structures north and south of the orphanage – small hotels and modest huts alike – had been completely shattered by the waves.

Only 30 of the 102 children of Grace Home were on the compound during the school holiday period. Those who had relatives – cousins, uncles, aunts or the random combinations that comprised so many families in the northeast – were away from the orphanage; it would be weeks before their tsunami fates would be fully learned.

There were, however, moments of panic on the peaceful grounds that morning. One of the children, 17-year-old Sudanthy, was battling the flu and had overslept. When the first wave flooded the orphanage, Sudanthy awoke to the sound of water, thinking at first that someone was washing the walls of Grace Church with a loud hose.

That thought vanished quickly. The small room she shared, a space barely able to fit four bunk beds and a single cabinet, filled with water. Sudanthy scrambled to the top bunk in search of air, and struggled to pry open a nearly-submerged door.

From the nearby main hall, she heard facility manager Rev. Gnanapragasm call her name, shouting to find her, and she fought harder to open the door. When a big enough space to squeeze through opened, she slipped off the bunk, into the water, and swam away from the now-receding waves to the church.

She, and everyone else at Grace, ran inland before the second wave blasted through the trees. They remained, for long after, near the front gate, as far away from what they would call "Tsunami Beach" as they could get.

***

The historic disaster was, in many ways, just one more challenge for an already beaten region. Some of the children told legends, born of myth and adopted by experience, claiming that the tsunami was itself just a signal, foreshadowing the day when four "Dark Knights" would visit the land, symbols seen as messengers of a pending apocalypse.

For many, the tsunami seemed the final tragedy of a life mired in misery. Not long after the disaster, the Grace girls welcomed a new classmate at Methodist Girls College, an orphan child who had lost so much already, and for whom the disaster took what little she had left.

Born and raised in Batticaloa, 15-year-old Ramiya was familiar with loss. An uncle of hers died in the war during the late 1980s; shortly after she was born, Ramiya's father was killed while looking for food in the jungle. That same year, her mother succumbed to a lifetime of illness, leaving Ramiya with an ailing grandmother, who herself became a widow five years later.

When the waves came, Ramiya, her grandmother and neighbors climbed to the roof of their Batticaloa home to escape the flood. She watched the water recede, the brief calm before unstoppable, crashing waves washed over the village, taking away her younger relatives.

Ramiya was knocked out, yet witnesses told her how she held on to the trunk of a tree through sheer, barely conscious, survival instinct. When she regained awareness, she was floating among several dead bodies.

With neither a single possession in the world nor a family member to love, Ramiya gave in: She let go of the tree and left her fate in the hands of the disaster.

She was spared, and pulled from the water by another survivor. Connections were made by a local church, and Ramiya was taken to Trincomalee, where she would live and learn at Methodist Girls College, balancing daily words of encouragement from teachers against nightly dreams dominated by death.

Few, if any, tsunami survivors did not lose a loved one, friend, or child to the tsunami. Those who lived, however, had little time to grieve; the total impact of the disaster grew more severe with each passing day. Supplies were destroyed, transportation prevented, the community a broken skeleton of what it had been.

At the Alles Gardens camp next to Grace, elder fisherman Kunam and his family were among those able to escape the pounding waves, leaving everything behind in a scramble for safety. When he returned to the camp, Kunam found the remains of his fishing boat, shattered into pieces, and wondered how he would feed his family. Nearly a dozen fishermen lived in Alles Gardens, their daily catch supporting the small community both as food and at market. Their existence relied upon getting out to sea – for those still willing to head into the waves in the days and weeks following the tsunami – but only a fraction of their engines and boats survived the disaster.

Kunam often looked at the sea in the days following the tragedy, frustrated by the lucrative tuna season that was passing by uncaught. They would have to start again, he knew, to rebuild what little they had, but they weren't certain how to start, or what could be done.

"I went to start cleaning up, but there was nothing to clean," Kunam said. "Everything was cleaned by the waves."

***

Rushing through a devastated town to Trincomalee General Hospital, Dr. Sathaharan ("Satha") Sundaralingam realized it would be days before he left the facility. (For months after, he worked 80 or more hours a week treating non-stop patients.)

"There were so many deaths," said Satha, who had seen plenty since joining the hospital staff in 2000. "It was so tragic."

The greater tragedy he spoke of was not just the deaths caused by the initial blast of the tsunami, but those who might have been spared in the aftermath.

"We could have saved 30 lives," he said of a particularly frustrating period following the tragedy, when too many obstacles prevented injured patients from getting to the hospital, or for doctors to reach

Leonard David, principal of St. John's Academy in Batticaloa, explains how a simple well was fashioned from parts including a wheel from a tuk-tuk, and rubber gaskets made from the soles of old sandals. In the aftermath of the tsunami, David organized students – many of whom were former child soldiers – to help remove the dead from the streets of "Batti."

those in need. Access to Trinco General was a challenge ordinarily to those in remote, isolated villages; the tsunami made it all but impossible for patients – or doctors – to reach the facility. Those who did added to the overwhelming caseload facing an already taxed staff. (Assistance included a retired, 70-year-old, surgeon who reported to the hospital and, for several weeks, averaged 30 or more daily surgeries.)

The day of the disaster, Satha said, was just the beginning. Immediate care was given for countless broken bones, trauma and shock. In the days and weeks that followed, health conditions in and around Trinco gave birth to near-epidemic levels of respiratory infections, bronchitis, malaria and other diseases. On the heels of an emergency room crisis, Satha said the community would feel the impact of the tsunami for months, perhaps years.

"After that, there were many people affected psychologically," said Satha, a native of Trincomalee. In a country that already posted one of the highest suicide rates in the world, there was a dramatic increase in people taking their own lives – some inspired by survivor's guilt after losing loved ones to seemingly random selection. Alcoholism became problematic for many in the northeast; civil order (as much as existed in a region that survived two decades of civil war) gave way to desperate looting, assaults, and other behaviors of those who lost hope.

Satha and the region's doctors struggled to treat those injured by the tsunami; other, equally pressing chores needed to be addressed in every community along the coast. In Batticaloa, Rev. Jeyanesan's St. John's Center became a pivotal base for projects to repair and restore a community. Those in leadership roles included the school's principal, Leonard David.

One priority was to take care of the dead, the hundreds of bodies in streets, homes, fields or wherever the tsunami left them; disposal would have to be done by whatever means necessary. David would spend weeks doing little else, assisted by a team of students, some of whom were former child soldiers with the LTTE.

Born near Colombo, David, 42, was a lifelong Sri Lankan, save for a seven-year stint as an aid worker in Saudi Arabia. He returned to his native land to work first with the International Red Cross before accepting Jey's offer at St. John's, where he managed the school and training center. (Since the opening of Grace, David spent part of his time in Trinco, guiding the still-in-development operations.)

The tsunami spared David's family; the waves did not reach the inland home he shared with his wife and three children, a pleasant house on a quiet street in an elevated section of Batticaloa. (With similar disbelief to Hiram Labrooy's, David doubted at first the cries that the sea water was coming in. "I never heard of such a thing," he said, assuming it must be another problem entirely.) He drove his motorbike toward the beach, just far enough to see dying fish littering the road; he turned and rode uphill before the second blast came, and he watched the deadly waves in all their sheer power.

At St. Johns, David, spoke with local officials, community leaders and other churches that were launching recovery operations. Those in authority had a daunting task facing them, and David wondered how long it would take to restore order, to come together as a community.

David assembled an informal team, and prepared to address those who still lay victim to the disaster. Tools were gathered at St. Johns, brought in from wherever the tsunami had casually tossed them, and teams were sent to scout the streets of Batticaloa. He saw how quickly the distinctions of being Tamil or Singhalese, Muslim, Buddhist or Hindu were forgotten. Working with a common purpose, David and a crew of students, soldiers, fishermen and others began the somber detail of removing the dead.

Among the volunteers he supervised included a reliable, consistent presence: dozens of former child soldiers. "We were running a program for ex combatants," David said. "Together we went and cleared the roads and all those bodies." (Since the cease fire agreement was signed, St. John's included more than 400 "ex combatants" in its training courses, the majority of whom did not return to battle.)

The detail continued for several weeks. In some cases, the bodies were too beaten, damaged or diseased to be safely removed. The

Another lousy day in paradise: The historic tsunami has made a bad situation all the more tragic. Makeshift camps (above) were formed by those fleeing villages destroyed by war or nature. (Below) Boys will be boys, and games of cricket will be played with homemade bats, on fields littered with the aftermath of destruction.

decaying corpses posed a health risk to the community-at-large, and somber cremations were conducted in lieu of proper burials. David recalled a single day, among many similar, which included the burning of 11 bodies, including two children.

"There was no option, they could not be carried, they could not be moved from where they were," David said.

When he thought the worst was over, David and others looked at the basic functions of the town, and what it would take to repair the already-struggling infrastructure. They discovered a well that supplied drinking water to a small village, which was producing a foul, blackish liquid. Further investigation revealed, at the bottom of the pit, the decaying corpse of a child.

The days were divided, David said, between grieving with friends and family – he did not know a single family that hadn't paid a human price to the disaster – and trying to prevent additional lives from being lost. David regretted missing the funeral of a friend's daughter, as he was needed elsewhere to help another family remove the body of a lost loved one.

***

The scientific community labeled it the Sumatra-Andaman earthquake, a massive undersea eruption that gave rise to a series of tsunami waves. The event of December 26, 2004 was the most devastating tsunami of all time, and one of the 10 deadliest natural disasters in recorded history. Primarily impacting Indonesia, Sri Lanka, Thailand and India, damage and death reached as far as the eastern coast of Africa, more than 5,000 miles away (a span twice the width of the continental United States) from the epicenter.

The size and scope of the disaster – an earthquake measuring 8.9 on the Richter scale, waves up to 80 feet high traveling more than 600 miles per hour when they hit Indonesia – stunned the world as stories emerged from those who survived.

Those statistics would take months to be confirmed. Reports during the first 24 hours after the disaster underestimated the extent of the damage, announcing that an estimated 4,000 Sri Lankans were killed that day; the final tally, in reality, reached Rev. Jeyanesan's prediction of 40,000 killed. All told, more than 220,000 deaths in 11 countries were attributed to the tsunami, and millions were displaced from their homes.

In Trinco, the news came in slowly, digested each day by those who wondered about their survival until the next morning, who waited to learn if their family had fallen victim to the tsunami. For weeks after, Hiram Labrooy spent his nights at Grace Care Center, sleeping on the floor of the makeshift pharmacy, waking up early to cycle home and spend time with his family before returning to Grace for another day's work.

His mother scolded him, telling him it was foolish to return to some place so close to the water, so close to another disaster that was feared by a nation.

"My mom said I was crazy," Labrooy said. "'If another tsunami comes, you will be killed,' she said. I told her there was more that I could do at Grace. There were no males there, and there are robbers who would steal or misuse the girls."

Labrooy, the children and Grace staff subsisted on carefully rationed bread and dry curry. The number of mouths to feed grew as the 30 girls who were on campus the day of the tsunami were joined, a few each day, by the 73 children whose safety was unknown at first. Labrooy and the staff of Grace considered themselves fortunate: On January 10, 2005, less than two weeks after the tsunami, the last of the Grace girls made it safely back to the orphanage.

No matter where they were at the time of the disaster, along the coast in small villages that suffered countless casualties, all 103 of the children survived.

"No one died from Grace," Labrooy said. "No one got badly hurt. Because of that, we don't care about the things getting damaged."

Labrooy and other orphanage staff members began the chore of picking up after the disaster. Although the buildings remained largely intact, the tsunami took with it most of the beds, furniture, linen, mattresses, cooking supplies and what few items of clothing the children owned. They would, again, start from scratch.

Efforts to rebuild or repair Trincomalee were handicapped by a host of problems. Power was out, safe drinking water was unavailable. Grace Care Center and its staff and friends (a crew of California doctors were on site within three days of the disaster, and Grace hosted a steady stream of visitors for months) turned their attentions to what could be done outside of the orphanage gates.

"We were okay, but there are still needs," said Labrooy. "Our neighbors around this place, the fishermen, the people affected by the war, they are depressed."

It was a different sense of loss, Labrooy said, from having to start a new life due to the war. Just one year earlier, the cease fire allowed Sri Lankans in the north and east a small sense of hope, of reclaiming lost lives.

"Now, they have lost everything to the tsunami," Labrooy said. "It's sad to say that someone does not have even a plate or a cup to drink water. It's just sad. I don't know how long it will take them to get back to a normal life."

Priorities changed in Trinco, and all of Sri Lanka. In the immediate aftermath of the tsunami, government security forces often worked side-by-side with members of the Tamil Tigers to deliver relief supplies to remote areas. In Batticaloa, Rev. Jey and Leonard David distributed essential plumbing, carpentry and masonry supplies, given to those in need regardless of religion or ethnicity, distributed by improvised partnerships of all manner of Sri Lankans.

"We will make it through this," David said not long after the tsunami, with an emphasis on the plural, collective population, a pledge that Labrooy agreed was the only hope for a beaten nation.

"We all have to get together and work hard for the poor," Labrooy said. "Forget the race and religion misunderstandings; share whatever you have, share love."

Some held out hope that, as the weeks went by, the tsunami might inspire Sri Lanka to echo what post-tsunami recovery inspired in

Indonesia. The Aceh province had been torn by civil conflict between the Sumatran government and an Islamic resistance group, the Gerakan Aceh Meredeka ("Free Aceh Movement"), which had been fighting for independence since 1976 (about the same time as the formation of the LTTE). When the tsunami devastated the peninsula, a ceasefire was immediately put in place; eight months later, the opposing sides reached a truce that held through the early years of recovery.

Many hoped a similar resolve might be found in a newly appreciative Sri Lanka.

"The tsunami taught us a lesson," Labrooy said. "It made things so much different. Before, the Sinhalese hated the Tamil, the Christian hated the Muslim; but the tsunami made so much damage for everyone that people all joined together and didn't care about race or religion. With love, you can make an enemy hug you. The tsunami is finished; we must forget it and hope that nothing like that happens again."

In the early months of 2005, the world sympathized with Sri Lanka's tsunami survivors; often unaware of the challenges they had faced for years. Grace Care Center founder Eric Parkinson called the disaster, "Par for the course" in the lives of the orphan children he'd come to consider his own. "These kids have spent their entire lives in war. They saw their parents butchered in front of them, their mothers raped. They've never known any other reality."

To the children of Grace and the people of Trincomalee, the tsunami was in many ways just another disaster, but it may have been one that offered the first common bond they'd ever known.

"We were fighting the war for 20 years," Labrooy said. "It is a battle you cannot win: If you win anything, you will only make someone hate you, and then there will be a day when they will win."

What's a Good Price for a Coconut Scraper?

She was standing by herself, all 25 pounds of her, screaming her little head off: Too obedient to move from where she was told to wait; too scared to stop the tears.

Other than the sad (but loud) crying, it was a rare moment of relative peace and quiet at Grace Care Center. Earlier, we waved good-bye to the girls, nearly 100 students packed into a sluggish but determined bus headed for school. The day care children were just starting to arrive, about 60 pre-schoolers from nearby camps and villages ready for a day of early lessons, a healthy meal, some exercise and a relatively cool nap.

Most of the visitors were still in the dining area, finishing breakfast and making plans for the day. I excused myself to go take pictures of the arriving kids, some of whom I'd met in their classroom the day before. I walked through the main hall, and saw the young girl standing at the other end, framed in the doorway and crying her eyes out.

It was the first time at day care for Danushi, a 3-year-old from the neighboring Alles Gardens camp for displaced families. A miscommunication of some sort left her waiting alone by the entrance. When I saw her, she had been there for however much time it takes a scared 3-year-old to start crying, which isn't very long.

"Hello," I said, both to the child and in hopes that another adult was within earshot (not that someone wouldn't have heard the kid by then). I walked slowly toward her, not wanting to further frighten an already upset little girl. I picked her up, offering comfort through hugs and whispered words of encouragement.

Her crying subsided, and little hands found comfortable places around my shoulders. The tears went away, but an obvious sniffle remained, with labored breathing and congestion. Looking her over more carefully, I saw that the insides of her forearms were dotted with infections.

"I know some people who would just love to meet you," I said. We walked toward the kitchen to see who was still around, and found a half-dozen of our mostly-medical crew still finishing their tea.

"Hey guys," I couldn't resist asking: "Is there a doctor in the house?"

The first to move, appropriately, was Bonnie Sowa, an emergency room pediatrician from Ann Arbor. Within a minute, we were seated in a semi-private corner, Danushi on my lap facing Sowa for a gentle examination. She definitely had a cold, but not pneumonia (a practical concern given the rates of respiratory illness in the camps). She had a staph infection, which caused the welts and boils on her arms. Bonnie administered ointment, and a child's dose of liquid medicine. We alerted the staff that, before going home that afternoon, Danushi should have more medicine from the bottle we placed in the refrigerator.

The patient seemed happy, relatively speaking. She was no longer crying, but wasn't quite smiling at the world just yet. By then, dozens of children filled the classroom with smiles and giggles, and Danushi found the comfort of being surrounded by people her own size.

I was away from Grace until returning for a late lunch, and made my way to the dining area in hushed, tip-toe fashion. Near the end of a row of children who lay napping under gentle ceiling fans, Danushi's head lifted slightly; she greeted me with one of the cutest little-kid smiles I'd ever seen. I made my way to her and whispered "hello," which brightened her eyes all the more.

Over the next few days, I made a point of being near the entrance when the day care kids arrived, and we found time for a few slow walks around the driveway. Danushi wasn't a talkative child by nature – compared to at least one day-care classmate, a beaming little boy who took every opportunity to babble excitedly at me, the language barrier holding no restriction over his enthusiasm – but she seemed to enjoy sitting quiet and close to me while the class sang songs to visitors.

By Friday, Sowa thought Danushi should have at least one dose of medicine over the weekend, and Grace's refrigerator kept cool what a camp *home could not. Surrounded by the peace and hope found on the Grace property, it was sadly easy to forget the lack of resources for so many outside of the Grace walls. Even before the tsunami multiplied their number, thousands of people in the north and east lived far below even the most basic "poverty level" standards. A refrigerator wasn't a possibility, even if they could fill its shelves.*

Early Saturday morning, I borrowed Hiram Labrooy's services as a translator to deliver the medicine to Danushi. Outside the swinging gate at the entrance to Grace, we turned the corner into the four adjoining acres of the Alles Gardens community.

In the five weeks since the tsunami, families had returned to the property, bringing tents, tarps, poles and whatever could be found to – once again – start building a new life. Near a communal water supply, Danushi's family – her mother, grandfather and infant brother – lived in a shelter built of black plywood and blue tarp affixed to lengths of branch. Two short panels of wood formed a semi-enclosed "ell" next to the entrance, a patio suitable for entertaining guests.

Labrooy introduced me and explained our visit: A doctor at Grace had looked at the child, and thought she should take the medicine we brought. Someone was sent to fetch Danushi from where she was playing with other children. She was walked by an adult, hand-in-hand, back toward us; stopping first at the water pump to clean her face before slipping into another tent for a relatively fresh sari before meeting her guests.

The smile was familiar, at first. Some things are typical of all kids, however: The sight of the medicine seemed to alarm Danushi. She backed away, and some sniffling threatened to bring back the familiar tears of a scared little girl.

Anticipating this, Danushi's mother produced a few precious pieces of candy, which she discreetly slipped into my hand to give to my little friend. When I held up the candy, Danushi stopped wailing, sniffled one last time, and mumbled something while accepting the treat.

The adults laughed, the sort heard at things that only kids might say. "Okay," she had said after taking the candy: "I'll stay now."

We visited for a while, and Danushi took my hand to walk our group back across the camp toward Grace. Kunam, an elder of the camp, joined us for our walk; the visit drew the interest of others as the morning's social event for the community.

It was gratifying that a small attempt to help one child was appreciated, but the enormity of the situation remained a tragic frustration: Fishermen without boats, mothers unable to feed families, children without the most basic resources for health care, an education or the expectation that their lives might improve.

At the entrance to the camp, a pair of 50-gallon tankards had been placed by a tsunami-inspired relief agency. As we said our good-byes, I watched a little boy, perhaps five years old, fill a small plastic bottle with water. He ran the bottle back to his tent.

After a week of watching doctors and others reach out to those in need, I'd seen that assistance didn't work by providing answers as much as by asking questions. What did these families need, I asked Kunam, to make things a little better?

Water pots, he said, without hesitation. While Hiram translated, Kunam waved his arms and pointed to the little boy, who was back to draw another small bottle's worth of water from the source.

Alles Garden was completely washed away by the tsunami. Those who survived and remained did so with just the clothes on their back. When their homes were blasted ashore or washed to sea, everything inside went with them, including the most basic cookware or kitchen equipment.

The relief agency that left the tankards of water (which were periodically filled) did so, Kunam said, with little communication. In an attempt to reach as many survivors as possible, those volunteers delivered quantities of clean water to as many camps as they could.

The people of Alles Gardens, however, had no method of getting the water to their tents, or keeping it somewhat cool.

"It sounds simple," Labrooy said of Kunam's request. "But no one looked into that." Water pots would be a great help, he said: Those, and coconut scrapers.

A little pre-schooler named Danushi (front and center) smiles on the trail leading to her new home in February 2006. Having lost their home to the tsunami, Danushi and her family stayed in the Alles Gardens camp for internally displaced refugees, where she joined the day care program at Grace Care Center. A year later, her family had was able to find a more substantial home further inland.

Learning to help: Although an international relief agency placed a tankard of water near a camp for displaced families, getting the water back to their shelter had to be done in patient fashion, such as a little boy (above) making multiple trips to fill a small beverage container. The author, with village elder Kunam (below), helped obtain water pots – and coconut scrapers – for families living next to Grace Care Center. (Photo by Hiram Labrooy)

My next question was for Labrooy, my guide for local shopping:
"So, what's a good price for a coconut scraper?"

That afternoon, Labrooy and I headed downtown to purchase (among other things) 26 water pots and coconut scrapers, one for each family unit living in Alles Gardens. A decent scraper, I learned, was a stool with a circular blade poking from the end, upon which the coconut is impaled and spun, its shavings dropping into a cooking pan.

The streets of Trinco were typical of a market Saturday, with pedestrians fighting for walking paths among bicyclists and cows; the tin-speaker sounds of beeping tuk-tuks were heard as they jostled back and forth on the narrow roads. Business at the fish market was slow: The tsunami packed the one-two punch of first destroying the boats and then dramatically altering marine life cycles, a disruption that would take months to stabilize.

We parked the van and ventured into one store after another. No single vendor in the small, general merchandise stores carried sufficient quantities of either item. Also, Labrooy was often skeptical of the quality, pointing out the flaws of inferior scrapers where the blade was likely to snap off easily, or the stool legs were unsteady. The water pots also came in a range of value, with certain shapes and metal better than others at keeping water cool against daily 100-degree temperatures. Labrooy was a determined customer; thrusting back questionable merchandise and heading for the door before being begged to reconsider, perhaps look at other samples. Boys were sent on bicycles to fetch additional scrapers – one eager kid returned with eight stools stacked and tied to the rear wheel frame of his bike. (Those, I decided, we definitely bought.)

We made one final stop, for which Labrooy's native savvy turned into typical helpless male: He had less of an idea than I did of a suitable toy for Danushi. We poked around aimlessly in a few stores before settling on a simple, stuffed teddy bear, assuming that the classics still worked.

Over my remaining days at Grace, I had occasion to venture into the camp – walking Danushi home from day care or interviewing Kunam about his tsunami experiences – and was able to see pots keeping cool water in tents or women twirling coconuts from small wooden stools.

By the time we left, Danushi's cold was all but gone, just another childhood bout with an ordinary illness. Others would come and go, with or without a brief visit from a western friend, or the silly gift of a teddy bear that would be kept in its plastic wrap. She didn't want to remove the wrapping and "ruin" the toy. It was, I was told, the most luxurious present she'd ever been given.

"He is a foreign man; he is surrounded by the sound, the sound
Cattle in the marketplace, scatterings and orphanages
He looks around, around; he sees angels in the architecture
Spinning in infinity, he says 'Amen' and 'Hallelujah.'"
– "You Can Call Me Al," Paul Simon

Chapter 5
Seven Acres of Hope

Risa Sharpe may have empathized with the children of Grace Care Center better than most – if not all – of the visitors in February 2005. They shared a feeling understood only by witnesses and survivors.

"There's a moment when you think you're going to die," Sharpe said. "This is it; your world is coming to an end."

Five weeks after the tsunami, that certainty of death remained a fresh memory to many Sri Lankans; for Sharpe, it was reminiscent of a September morning a few years earlier, when she emerged from a subway tunnel at Fulton Street in lower Manhattan.

"My office was in the south tower; my building was the second one hit," said Sharpe, employed by investment banker Morgan Stanley, tenants of the 83rd floor of the World Trade Center.

Sharpe found kindred spirits in northeast Sri Lanka, with common visual memories from opposite sides of the planet. In New York City on Sept. 11, 2001, or the day after Christmas in Sri Lanka three years later, the specifics differed but the images were the same: People running through the streets, screaming, crying, in search of lost loved ones; "Body parts laying on the ground, death all around, and the explosions," said Sharpe. The glass windows of the tower's lower floors gave in to the heat and pressure generated from above; from across the street, she heard the bursting glass of hundreds of windows making a sharp, popping sound, echoed throughout the concrete canyons as if the neighborhood was under small-arms attack.

The third-world poverty in northeast Sri Lanka was further impacted when the tsunami destroyed boats and disrupted ocean life. Fishing is the leading source of Trinco's economy, with one of the world's deepest natural harbors and pivotal access to trade routes. Fishermen struggled to make ends meet until they could return to the sea that both provided for and took from them.

"For a minute there," she said, "I was afraid for my life."

Time loses meaning in the wake of such overwhelming shock; clocks and calendars move at a different pace when people hold their breath in anticipation. Sharpe joined a city's population that drifted half-conscious through the weeks and months that followed the tragedy, losing track of how much time passed. During her days in Trincomalee, she often referred to Sept. 11 as "two years ago," when more than three had passed since America was attacked.

"They feel unsafe," Sharpe said. "They're waiting for the next wave; I was waiting for the next plane. We all felt like sitting ducks."

The aftermath was equally unsettling; accepting the loss of family and friends amid daily, visual reminders of death and destruction. Sri Lanka's coastlines were littered with damaged boats and broken buildings; in New York, a steady cloud of dust hung over the skyline for months, the final fires not extinguished until the following year.

Both Sharpe and the children had a front-row, first-hand look at images that were known to the world, seen on television and the Internet by an unprecedented global audience. When the tsunami captured international attentions on par with the global community that watched the collapse of the Twin Towers, Sharpe was in Alabama, visiting her large ("very large") family for the holidays. She didn't immediately watch the non-stop reports on television – the family holiday included many smaller children who were spared from the horrifying images – she desperately sought out information when she returned to New York. As exotic as the locations shown may have been, the human suffering made a particular connection with Sharpe.

"I woke up and said, 'I've got to go.' Something was driving me," Sharpe said. "I said a prayer that morning: 'If I'm meant to go, show me the way.' The door opened the very next day."

Sharpe sent out inquiries to agencies she assumed would be gathering resources for assistance: Save the Children, the Red Cross, UNICEF. She asked co-workers in her company's relocated New Jersey offices if they knew of a similar organization. The words "Sri Lanka" caught the

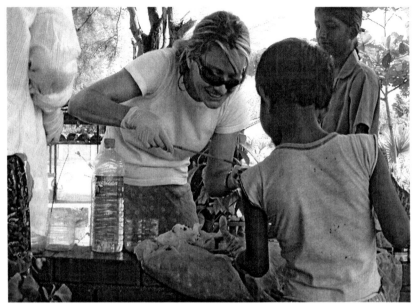

Profiles in dignity: Of all the VeAhavta visitors in early 2005, Risa Sharpe (above) might have best understood the trauma felt by tsunami survivors. In late 2001, Sharpe worked for New York investment banker Stanley Morgan, and watched the second plane hit her building, the south tower of the World Trade Center, during the Sept. 11 terrorist attacks on America. (Below) The residents of Trincomalee's coastal villages were left to pick up the pieces in the wake of the disaster. Rebuilding their lives was, first, a matter of finding the resources to build again, then waiting for disrupted supply channels to allow that effort to succeed.

ears of Romesh Gunaratnam, whose brother, Naresh, was a doctor in Ann Arbor who worked with an orphanage in that country.

Sharpe contacted Gunaratnam in Michigan, who invited her to join a team of mostly medical professionals affiliated with St. Joseph Mercy Hospital. Of the group, only Gunaratnam had been to the orphanage before the tsunami, and he enthusiastically described to Sharpe the needs of Grace Care Center, the relationships between the girls and the community, the challenges that faced them even before the tsunami.

It was the answer to Sharpe's prayer, a personal, one-on-one chance to provide assistance that couldn't be done long distance. In New York, she'd learned the value of community in matters of recovery, and thought she could offer some help.

"I'm never trying to say I know what these girls went through," Sharpe said, "but they need to feel safe, and I connected with that. That's the one thing we can give these girls."

Two weeks later, Sharpe met a dozen volunteers at JFK International Airport; 48 hours after that she was at Grace Care Center. The group carried minimal personal luggage yet tested the airline restrictions with baggage stuffed with medical supplies, gifts, donations and, forming a particularly clumsy package to transport, several wheelchairs. One of the travelers described the team's appearance as resembling, "The world's strangest rock band on tour." (The hand-carried method of delivering supplies worked. A substantial amount of materials sent to Sri Lanka from throughout the world would remain in Colombo warehouses for months; some of which became a topic of political and civil debate in the months ahead.)

Along with supplies, Sharpe came with another addition to the team, a trauma counselor she spoke with while researching her trip, Cheri Lovre, who linked with the growing group at JFK after flying in from Oregon. Twelve relative strangers became, within a few days, a cooperative group with a common purpose.

At Grace, Sharpe and Lovre undertook a psychological assessment of the children, expecting to find the scars of recent emotional trauma on their souls. There was plenty of evidence of that: The children made drawings of people and houses, the families obliterated by blue crayon waves washing over the image.

Other, more disturbing problems threatened the mental health of the children, discoveries made by Sharpe and Lovre that came alongside lessons learned by medical, social, educational and other studies. Some of the drawings and stories held images darker than even the tsunami: They'd seen death and rapes, beatings and suicides. One girl told them of losing a father to a cobra's poisonous bite; another became an orphan when her father was killed by soldiers who bludgeoned him to death.

The same post-traumatic shock that loses track of time created, Lovre told Sharpe, a "shutting down" of part of the brain. Before the children of Grace could continue their standard education, they would need to come to terms with a lifetime of suffering.

On a beach near Trincomalee, Sharpe played with girls whose brains fought to forget what their hearts couldn't, a feeling she understood all the more since coming to Grace Home. It was no longer an image on a television, a report in a newspaper.

"I was afraid I wouldn't add any value," Sharpe said, a fear shared by many of the travelers. "I found a place that people are so passionate about, and I didn't know why at first. But the traumatic part, needing to feel safe, I connected there. That's one thing we can give the girls."

**

He was the one who started it, but Mohammed Nadeemullah – "Nadeem" as he was known – didn't get to enjoy the dancing party. The 48-year-old doctor, originally from Karachi, Pakistan, was too exhausted from long days working the Mercy Mobile Medical Clinic. When a talent show ended and the main hall of Grace Care Center was turned into a dance club – entertainment that began with a simple cadence beat upon a drum by Nadeem – the doctor was soon seen on a cot in an adjacent hallway, fast asleep.

He was near the point of exhaustion. Nadeem and a small medical team, including emergency room pediatrician Bonnie Sowa, started

International house calls: Doctors from Michigan who made the trip to Trincomalee in early 2005 included (above) Mohammad Nadeemullah, who spent most of his days traveling to remote villages with the mobile clinic, travels that included a ferry ride to Kinniya. (Below) Bonnie Sowa made countless friends while working clinic duty, a service that sent her on a dead-of-night search to try and save a baby she thought was dying. (Photo courtesy Bonnie Sowa.)

their days early, departing from the orphanage at sunrise to visit remote villages for clinics that lasted well into evening. Dozens of patients were seen each day as they roamed the countryside surrounding Trincomalee.

Nadeem's medical practice in Brighton, Michigan, was affiliated with Gunaratnam's St. Joseph Mercy Hospital. When he saw and heard the tsunami reports, the images reminded him in many ways of his native country, where he lived until age 29 before moving to Ann Arbor, Michigan. He prayed for those in need, of course, but when he learned that a team from his hospital's network was forming for a mission to Trincomalee, he knew that human – not divine – action was needed.

"I had given up praying," Nadeem said, "or asking God to do this or that." He was compelled to be part of whatever answers God might provide.

From a medical standpoint, that solution was decidedly a hands-on experience during days lasting 15, 16 or more hours on the road. The van's arrival in a village was, typically, first spotted by an alert boy on a bicycle, who pedaled enthusiastically around town announcing the news. By the time Hiram Labrooy parked the vehicle and the doctors set up shop – in abandoned roadside shacks, a classroom or other unused structure – dozens of ill or injured souls stood waiting for treatment. The doctors often helped, with medication or advice that would put a patient on a proper course of treatment; sometimes, sadly, Nadeem was limited in what he could do. A man with a dangerously low heart rate suffering chest pains would, in America, be put on an IV, given nitro glycerin and transported to a hospital; in a remote village in Sri Lanka, the man was added to a list of patients needing help from a better-equipped agency. Nadeem hoped the referrals would be answered in sufficient time.

While not serving clinic duty, Nadeem joined the volunteer crew on other appointments, some fact-finding, others that offered indirect assistance. In Kinniya – a village south of the harbor from Trinco – the team met with an Italian medical group that built a temporary, M*A*S*H-style tent facility to replace a tsunami-destroyed hospital.

Along with much discussion of possible cooperative projects, Nadeem posed a simple question to one of the Italian doctors.

"How can we help you," Nadeem asked, kindness and compassion accenting his simple words. "What do you need?"

A specific piece of medical equipment was needed, he was told, a device easy to obtain in Italy or America, but not an item to be found in northeast Sri Lanka.

"We have an extra one," Nadeem said. "I will bring it to you." The next day, his clinic appointments included a brief stop in Kinniya to deliver on his promise. (Appreciation for the donation, the doctors said, was equally due to the question having been asked: What do you need? Nadeem was told of a well-meaning group of visiting doctors shortly after the tsunami who donated a machine that, sadly, the staff on hand was not familiar with, nor could the electrical standards accommodate the device.)

Some patients seen by Nadeem and Sowa couldn't be helped, at least not by doctors. A young woman entered the improvised examining room, perhaps 10 square feet with burlap sacks of rice lining the walls, carrying an infant who lay cushioned on a pillow: A baby girl, far too small even at 10 days old.

"This baby was not responsive at all, just totally out of it," Sowa said, thinking: "This baby is going to die." The newborn was dehydrated, was not taking or discharging liquids or foods, had an accelerated heartbeat, and her shallow breathing had slowed to dangerous levels by the time Sowa held the child.

The baby must be taken to the hospital, Sowa said; the van could take them immediately. Through an interpreter, the girl was told that the situation was critical.

The young mother, not much older than the senior Grace children, refused treatment, however: That was a decision for her husband. With a sense of duty-bound honor, she thanked the doctors and returned home with a dying child.

Unable to take other action immediately, Sowa finished the clinic that day, but couldn't stop thinking about the certain death awaiting the baby. Back at Grace, Sowa told Gunaratnam and VeAhavta president Eric Parkinson about her concerns. By Western standards, the baby would have been admitted with or without parental consent, a matter of life or death in which doctors must play advocate.

"That's my role," Sowa said of her American job in a pediatric emergency room, "to do everything in my power to take care of the child."

Parkinson agreed, and Sowa accepted the offer to take the van back out to the field. Into the evening rode Sowa, Labrooy and Nadeem, first stopping at a small pharmacy in Kinniya, where Sowa was stunned by the quantities of medication available at, compared to American standards, rock-bottom prices. "Oh look, they're having a sale," she said – and paid pennies for what would cost dollars in America, prices still out of reach for the majority of northeast Sri Lankans. Sowa paid $18 American dollars for medical supplies that would have cost more than $700 in the west.

Although they weren't certain where the baby and her young mother lived, they were determined that they could be found in the small village. The van was parked on a narrow dirt road in front of where the clinic was held; the group began knocking door-to-door, until they found the family – living just a few structures away from the clinic – in a single-room dwelling lit by a bare light bulb.

In that room they found the baby's parents, grandmother and, against all medical logic, a 10-day-old girl, "Practically come back to life." The baby was awake and alert, with most every vital sign within normal ranges.

It could be considered a miracle, but medical skepticism sent Sowa seeking other explanations, most found in the small, wrinkled grandmother, whose survival of 60 years of Sri Lankan life indicated knowledge and experience on par with sophisticated doctors from the west. Sowa learned that the aging matron took matters into her own hands and guided the baby through forced feedings that brought back her strength.

"That tells me there are a lot of wise people out here," Sowa said. The wisdom of the elderly was a commodity in Sri Lanka, practiced by determined souls making the most of limited resources, with little more than hard-earned experience to guide them.

***

When he agreed to join his wife on a two-week relief mission to Grace Care Center, one thing Lynn Helland feared was not being useful.

"I dreaded wasted time," said Helland, an attorney with the U.S. District Court in Detroit. "But there have been no spinning wheels."

Helland's wife, Dr. Cheryl Huckins, was among the majority of the traveling group who connected with what was assumed to be primarily a medical mission. He didn't want to just "tag along" or, as other non-doctors on the team also feared of their participation, get in the way of critical, life-saving efforts. Helland was willing to lend a hand, help assess the situations, or do whatever was needed when opportunities presented themselves.

Could he help build a boat house? Eric Parkinson asked Helland about picking up a hammer for a possible project that, on paper from a distance, could be a benefit to the local fishermen. As an economic indicator, the health of the fishing industry determined the well being of Trincomalee. The natural formations surrounding the peninsula of Trinco made a barrier against the roughest ocean, which kept relatively calm one of the world's deepest natural harbors. As a result, a variety of species populated Trinco's waters without pause in the calendar, the non-stop seasons allowed a year-round industry to flourish more consistently than anywhere else on the island.

After the tsunami, the head of a local fishing union told VeAhavta's visitors that marine biology was interfering with their industry. "There was very less fish," said Anandaperice, a local Justice of Peace and President of the Fisherman's Society of Trincomalee. "It is very hard to find any fish in the sea."

Boats for the fishermen: In February 2005, arrangements were made for VeAhavta to provide several boats to a local fishing union, many members of which lost their vessels to the tsunami. (Above, from left) Michigan attorney Lynn Helland, VeAhavta President Eric Parkinson and Hiram Labrooy discuss the proposal with local fishermen, who (below) accepted delivery of the boats in August 2005. The agreement included a provision that a portion of each day's catch would go to families in the camps near Grace Care Center.

The fishermen of Trinco tried, but with limited resources. Less than two months after the disaster rearranged nature's cycles, fishermen spent frustrating mornings searching the sea in vain. A crew of a dozen men routinely went to work each sunrise on the beach outside of Grace Care Center: One man steered a small boat to a distance of perhaps 100 feet from shore, dropping along the way a net that would be lugged and tugged ashore by two rows of men on the beach, who pulled in nets containing a fraction of what the same exercise brought two months earlier.

At first, the plan was to build a boat house to help a fishing union get back in business, but Parkinson and Helland quickly recognized that there were few boats left to make use of the facility. The beaches near Grace were representative of a lengthy coastline littered with broken vessels. The community maintained its industry as well as possible. Nature would readjust the fish populations in time, but basic supplies would be needed to take advantage of the bounty awaiting.

There's an old adage about giving a man a fish and feeding him for a day; teach him to fish and he will be fed him for a lifetime. An amendment to that philosophy was born at Grace Care Center: Give men boats, and help feed a village.

An offer was presented for VeAhavta to purchase boats and nets that would send the men back to the sea. In exchange, a portion of their daily catch would help feed the displaced families in Alles Gardens. After gathering estimates from local suppliers, funds would be found to buy and equip four fishing boats for use by one of the fishing unions.

Groups of fishermen and union officials paid a visit to Grace before an agreement was reached with Anandaperice and the Fisherman's Society of Trincomalee, a reputable collective that, among other criteria, counted among its membership a mix of Singhalese, Tamil and Muslim fishermen proportionate to Trinco's melting-pot population.

There was a lot at stake. Four men each would be able to work in the four boats supplied by VeAhavta, with the proceeds of a good day's catch spreading benefits throughout the economy. Anandaperice said use of the nets – an expense greater than the boat itself – dramatically increased the productivity, allowing a crew to net in three hours what would take dozens of men 10 hours or more to catch with hooks. Up to 500 kilograms of fish daily could be brought to shore per boat, to feed IDP camp families, to be sold downtown at market, or to be exported through an agent to Colombo, keeping the Union active as a distributor.

After an initial meeting with Anandaperice, Parkinson and Helland met with three members of the Fisherman's Society, seated at a dining table in Grace, the sounds of day care classroom activity on the other side of the room filling in the atmosphere. Labrooy, serving as translator, had been fighting a flu (driven by near-complete lack of sleep as the 10-day visit by this group of volunteers neared an end). Several times during the proceedings, Labrooy excused himself for a hurried, nausea-inspired dash to the restroom, returning minutes later to continue the dialogue.

The meeting concluded with promises that would be kept: The fishermen returned the next day with price quotes for boats, engines and nets, ready to sign a contract. Helland spent much of the previous evening seated in a relatively quiet corner of the main hall at Grace, a laptop computer perched on a wobbly stand while he typed out an agreement that would feed dozens of local families.

Before the contract was finalized and put into action, the document required approvals and additional approvals from various levels of government. The specifics of the contract bogged down, at times, with unexpected delays.

"Maybe giving away boats is more complicated than I thought it would be," Helland said of the obstacles. "The logistics were more difficult, but the bottom line is the same. We were trying to reach a meeting of the minds; we were trying to give them something, so it was especially easy to reach that meeting."

As an exercise in economics, Helland broke down the costs of the agreement that, once put into practice, would allow 20 or so families freedom from worrying about how they would feed their children: Apart from the time he and Parkinson spent with the fishermen, the cost of transportation, translating the two-page document and making copies came to about $6.80 American.

It was never about the money, though, and Helland and Parkinson knew that the project would only work with monitoring and sustained effort in Trinco. Long-distance assistance can provide funds, but relief work – long term – depends upon sustained work.

"It would be easier to buy the boats, turn them over and walk away," Helland said, but VeAhavta's habitual involvement would not allow that. Over the next few months, Labrooy reported the status of the fishing agreement. The project, as with most worthwhile efforts in Sri Lanka, required patience: suppliers struggled to fulfill the backlog of orders for vessels, engines, nets and other assets that had to be replaced in an environment where distribution channels were also slowly recovering from the disaster.

As with most projects launched at Grace that year, patience paid off. In August, Rev. Gnanapragasm said a solemn prayer during a ceremony on the beach. Firecrackers were lit, per age-old custom, and fishermen (and guests) enjoyed the maiden voyage of the Grace Care Center fleet of fishing boats. It was the best sort of celebration, a reward not given to a momentary, grand display of effort or generosity, but instead earned by a sustained involvement, a connection with people that didn't attempt to provide answers but instead asked simple questions: "How can we help you?"

The ceremony that put boats in the water and food on the table was witnessed by the usual assortment found at Grace; some children, the orphanage staff, a few American friends. By August 2005, the Grace community included a new group of residents, the start of a population known as Mercy Home, a residence for senior citizens whose collective history reflected the nation they called home.

A year earlier, the "elder orphanage" had been just another dream at Grace.

Dancing on the Beach

The tragedy was being told to Hiram Labrooy, who listened while a small, frail-looking woman shared her sorrow.

Labrooy considered the proper words for translation, anticipation that seemed to silence the ordinary, persistent sounds usually heard at Grace Care Center: The perpetual wash of the ocean and constant caw-ing of crows seemed, briefly, unheard.

Labrooy arranged for me to interview the woman, Valliyamma Tharmaligam (the motherhood-denoting suffix, "amma," a sadly ironic legacy). After brief introductions, we talked about the war's impact on her life. She began telling her story, often shifting uncomfortably on a bench, surrounded by the healthy vegetation that lined the entrance to Mercy Home, the recently opened elder residence on the orphanage property.

When the conflict started, Valliyamma was living with her husband and 10-year-old son, Manikarasa, in the low hills near Kandy; both she and her husband served on a tea plantation. Her small, sinewy arms bore evidence of plucking countless leaves over a lifetime, often earning two Rupees (two American cents) a day for her labor.

Her voice grew strained, anguished, angry. She illustrated the story with her hands and body; she raised her arm and swung it back in a slashing motion, a forefinger extended toward her neck. She started crying, shaking her head. There was a pause before Labrooy echoed her statements.

"When they started doing war in 1983," Labrooy shrugged, carefully finding the words. "Her son got his head chopped off."

It was men in uniform, she said, likely on the side of the government. Her small family was one of dozens living in cottages near the tea fields. Proximity to the jungle often made suspects of the innocent: The soldiers targeted young males, and on that day were dragging children out of their small homes. Some were beheaded with machetes.

She remembered the images, of the boy's head going to one side and the body another direction. Her memories were fleeting after that: She ran aimlessly, screaming, crying. She tripped and fell into a tree, breaking her teeth and facial bones (a memory consistent with her appearance).

If the sight of her son's beheading wasn't the most severe shock a human can experience, that condition was passed when she saw the boy's head mounted on the branch of a nearby, roadside tree.

("They do that to scare other people," Labrooy later explained.)

Valliyamma collected herself, clumsily wiped a twisted, arthritic hand across her eyes. Other American visitors were nearby, and nature's seeming silence allowed them to hear a story more disturbing than our combined experiences in Sri Lanka could have imagined. A physical therapist from Michigan, sitting at the base of a coconut tree, dropped her head into folded arms; a college student monitoring the video camera that recorded the interview removed the plug from his ear and walked away in disbelief. Valliyamma's weren't the only tears shed that day.

The sounds of Mercy Home came back to life; nature returned its soundtrack to the residence for destitute senior citizens that had been in operation just a few weeks. Among the first of the elders to be admitted, Valliyamma stood about 5 feet tall, and weighed perhaps 80 pounds. She claimed to be in her early 60s, although exact records for indentured hands at tea plantations are rarely available or accurate; the birth year entered in her file was an estimate, drawn from the shattered memories of both Valliyamma and her mother, Ponnamma Perumal. The two women were living together when they were brought to the elder home.

After witnessing her son's brutal death, Valliyamma was institutionalized for several years before being cast out into an impoverished society. Life didn't get any worse – not that it could – but it didn't improve: Her husband was killed, reportedly by troops from India during that nation's brief attempt at bringing order to Sri Lanka. What was left of her family sought refuge in the growing number of refugee camps in the north and east, a growing percentage of the country's population.

Among the first residents of Mercy Home, Valliamma barely survived
the years leading up to her joining the Grace family. After a youth spent
working on a tea plantation, she watched in horror as men in uniforms
killed her 10-year-old son. At Mercy Home, Valliamma enjoyed a renewed
sense of vitality and a place to call home, for both herself and her ailing
mother.

Lord, have Mercy: Against a backdrop of third world poverty, the grounds
of Mercy Home offered a peaceful place for destitute seniors to spend their
final days. Opened by VeAhavta in May, 2005, Mercy Home was soon filled
with dozens of elders, who formed a community with the children of Grace
Home.

Labrooy shook his head when he described how he found the two women – an octogenarian mother and a daughter approaching retirement age – fighting off stray dogs to defend their meager possessions: A small frying pan, a modest bag of rice and some salt to add to the meal.

"A dog came and was eating the rice," Labrooy said. "She chased it away and served the rice to her mother." The broken cottage they called home offered only partial shelter against the elements: There was no roof left on the small building. "In the daytime you can see the sun, and at nighttime you can see the moon," Labrooy translated Valliyamma's light-hearted description, himself recalling the sight of the women surviving in such conditions. "It was horrible," he sighed. "In my life I have never seen people living like that."

Labrooy contacted those who planned Mercy Home, who confirmed his belief that these two ladies should be among those who would live at Grace Care Center's newest provider of hope.

There was a rejuvenating quality to Mercy Home that instilled in its residents more than the planned "nursing home" envisioned – to provide rudimentary medical care for conditions resulting from years (decades) of exposure, malnourishment, disease and poverty. Ponnamma was unable to walk when she was first wheeled into Grace Care Center; within a few months, tentative steps were taken that, in time, became daily mobility. There was a stubborn strength among Sri Lanka's oldest survivors.

A community developed between the girls of Grace Home and the elders, whom they treated with the utmost respect. Routines developed: Tea times found teenage girls joining the elders for small talk, stories of school lessons and the contact that defines "family;" brief morning visits by playful children from the day care program effortlessly inspired smiles in faces and eyes that had seen Sri Lanka's troubled history first-hand.

During a return visit several months later, I joined a dozen or so elder men and women for an afternoon stroll on the beach. The sounds near the ocean were full of life, as were the seniors who looked upon the waves. If the orphan children of Grace Care Center offered a small sliver of hope for a nation's future, Valliyamma and the melting pot of Mercy Home's residents provided other forms of promise, a reminder that the tragedies of history can be survived.

Valliyamma stooped to pick up stray husks of coconuts littering the beach, shells left behind by crows that enjoyed their nourishment. She took a few running steps before happily throwing a football-shaped shell into the waves, for no other reason than to have some fun on the shore. I went to take her picture: She stood still, at first, a smile beaming from her broken mouth. Perhaps thinking I was recording moving images, she rocked and swayed with playful rhythm, dancing on the beach because she could.

"The best thing we can do is form a community to reach out.
All the money in the world won't float the boat.
It's human relationships that will."
— Eric Parkinson

Chapter 6
Mercy

Grace Care Center wasn't supposed to keep growing; at least, not according to Eric Parkinson's initial plans. Satisfied to watch Grace Home's population reach its capacity, Parkinson wasn't receptive, at first, to the next idea proposed by the energetic Sri Lankan minister, Rev. S. Jeyanesan.

"I thought it was going to stop at 100 kids," Parkinson said. "It would be an orphanage for 100 children, and that's where it would end. Then Jey mentioned to me a dream he had of an 'elder home.'"

Jeyanesan was, in effect, asking Parkinson to "do it again," and build a residence for destitute senior citizens.

"I treated it as a dream," Parkinson said. "I was thinking: That's your dream, I've dreamed enough."

The idea, however, was planted. Just as it was when Jeyanesan informed Parkinson that, yes, they would build an orphanage on a remote beach in Trinco, the "dream" of an elder's facility on the compound quickly became a plan to be realized.

There were countless obstacles to overcome before the first elder took up residence in Mercy Home, its evolution a checklist of notable progress and frequent setbacks. When Jeyanesan first presented the idea in 2003, Grace Home was well on its way to its 100-child capacity. Other programs at Grace, comparable to Rev. Jey's operations in Batticaloa, were up and running and the prospects seemed endless:

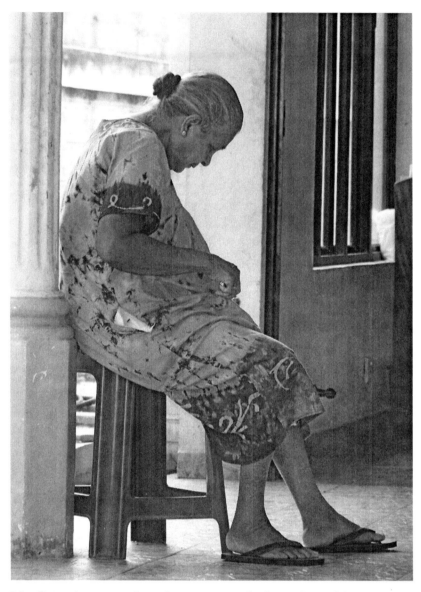

Mrs. Rajarathnam, a widow who was among the first to live at Mercy Home, soon began working in the kitchen, giving her a sense of ownership and stability. "God has placed me in a home full of loving people who care for and are very concerned about others," she said of the community at Grace Care Center.

The Vocational Training Center was launched in October 2003, and relative peace seemed ready to stay for a while. Parkinson understood that the elder home was a natural extension of Grace.

"The day care and widows empowerment projects started," Parkinson said. "The more I saw what was happening, and the more I got to know the kids, I wanted to do the elder home. There was a great need for it, and I thought we could pull it off."

The expected cost of the project seemed reasonable – approximately $140,000 to construct and equip the buildings that would house and care for up to 84 residents. Based on the relative ease (at least, in hindsight) with which Grace Care Center obtained its start-up costs, Parkinson was encouraged. In early 2004, VeAhavta announced plans and began raising funds for "Mercy Home," and a companion "Mercy Clinic" that would administer to residents and launch a mobile operation. Throughout 2004, the concept of Mercy Home was shaped as the seven barren acres became crowded with promise. It was an expansive period, fueled by the welcome silence of a cease-fire that lasted first for weeks, then months, with delicate hints of turning into actual peace.

The disaster that brought 2004 to an end further accented the need for sheltering destitute elders (along with the need for additional orphanages in northeast Sri Lanka). The tsunami left hundreds of thousands of children, widows and seniors with nowhere to turn. (The term "orphan" took on new meanings in the region: The children of Grace Care Center may not have lost both parents, although many had; the inability of what little family they had left to provide for them qualified the children as orphans, as it would a growing population of destitute elders who had no family to take care of them.)

Mercy Home's progress – under construction buildings with a still-incomplete floor plan at the time of the disaster – was stalled, but not abandoned after the tsunami. Included in the February, 2005 group of visitors were Michigan doctors Cheryl Huckins and Gina Amalfitano, who accepted Parkinson's invitation to help bring the facility's plan to reality. Huckins and Amalfitano recognized both the need and

Profiles in dignity: Born in 1920, Kanahasabai Sevasegaram (above) was a lifelong resident of Trincomalee before joining the Mercy Home community in 2007. Sevasegaram lost his two brothers, a brother in law, and three nephews to the conflict. (Photo by Hiram Labrooy). Thangarasa Valliyamma (below, right) worked at a tea estate until an armed group stormed the farm, shooting workers and burning their bodies. Thangarasa was among a few survivors who hid in the tea bushes for days before fleeing to safety. Sinnapillai Menake (left) is a widow who lived at St. John's in Batticaloa before joining Mercy Home in September 2005. After an accident, in which she lost part of her leg, doctors recommended her for residency at Mercy Home.

its severity, and embraced the challenge of managing the facility's completion and initial operations.

"There are tens of thousands of folks who have been living in displaced camps for 15 years or more," Amalfitano said. "The tsunami created more camps."

The elders from the already-struggling northeast were a tougher breed than many – because they'd had to be; those with more comfortable lives before the tsunami had more shocking adjustments to make. "People who weren't used to being displaced didn't have the coping skills for that situation," said Amalfitano, who previously went on medical missions to struggling communities in Mexico. The widespread poverty in Trincomalee and its surrounding areas was even more severe than she expected.

"Trinco's not a pretty place," Amalfitano shrugged, which made all the more impressive the environment she found at Grace Care Center: "A little Eden in the midst of squalor."

Mercy Home was planned under the expectation of largely bed-ridden residents with atrophied muscles, respiratory issues and other crippling byproducts of decades-long exposure to poverty and the elements. Those results were readily on display when the visiting doctors toured Trincomalee General Hospital. Huckins admired the efforts of medical workers in Sri Lanka while recognizing the limitations.

"They do so much with so little," Huckins said during her first visit to the bustling, central hospital that serviced the entire Trincomalee district, populated by hundreds of thousands of people living well below even the most generous standard for poverty. During a daytime visit, Trinco General's reception room was crowded with patients and loved ones who had traveled up to 100 kilometers – often on bicycles – to seek treatment.

Huckins also visited the one similar facility in Trinco for seniors, ironically found less than a half-kilometer down the road from Grace Care Center. A modest home operated by the Sisters of Mercy, where three nuns tended to three dozen mentally disabled, destitute adults.

There was a lot to be learned from the Sisters, and from the doctors

Huckins and Amalfitano consulted. Some cultural differences were found, and the expectations of Mercy Home were often adjusted. Staffing would be difficult to fulfill: Due to a severe shortage of health care providers, licensed nurses were required to work at the hospital, and were unavailable for employment at what would be considered a "private" home. To offset this hurdle, courses were held at the Vocational Training Center to teach some of the older Grace girls the basics of patient care.

"We had to adjust our expectations for the realities of a country in turmoil," Huckins said. "People don't travel late at night, so it wasn't feasible to have work schedules with shifts ending after 9 p.m. We also had to adapt time-off requests to fit with the cultural norm, yet still meet the needs of round-the-clock care. It was, and remains, an interesting exercise in problem solving."

The original concept of Mercy Home was, Amalfitano said, a hospice for, "Orphaned, impoverished elders of all backgrounds and faiths, facing the end of their lives. I envisioned something hospital-like, with frail and very sick elders who would need complete personal care."

Instead, those who would call Mercy "Home," although often suffering from chronic conditions, surprised American doctors, and even themselves.

***

During the early days of Sri Lanka's independence, those with means, education or position held the variations of political arguments to be expected of any newly-minted democracy. Particular to Sri Lanka were debates over whether or not their previous British rulers disproportionally favored the minority Tamils, a population that grew over the generations as British officials and plantation owners imported working class hands from the India's Tamil Nadu province. When the second half of the 20th Century welcomed Sri Lanka as a nation of its own, Tamils represented about one fourth of the country's total population.

Some British claimed that the Tamils were, on the whole,

Mercy Home resident Chandradasa, affectionately known as "Mr. Gandhi" for both his resemblance to the man of peace and his leadership, which helped Mercy Home develop beyond a residence for aging patients and into a vibrant community whose residents feel pride of ownership and long-sought after dignity.

better educated and worked harder, and rewarded that belief with administrative positions; in turn, the fledgling government included more than a few Tamils with significant titles. Conversely, Singhalese loyalists claimed that Tamils had been given preferential treatment under British rule, and that, as the majority, it was time for the Sinhalese language, customs and (in time) religion to take their rightful place as the island's dominant culture.

Those who came of age during the transitional 1960s and 1970s were fighting against forces not of their making, up to and including the inevitable war fueled by the ethnic division among politicians. Migration from one region to another did little to improve the stability of life for all citizens, as families were scattered around the island, returning many Sri Lankans to their ancestral, nomadic instincts. As the conflict grew, an increasing number of "bystanders" had their shops burned or looted; were attacked by mobs; or lost their modest livelihoods to the conflict. Some also learned to distrust lifelong friends – if they happened to be of a different ethnic background.

The hostilities that began in the late 1970s – officially called a "war" after 1983 – filled the small island with the natural byproducts of a 20-plus year conflict. By the 21st Century, the nation's youth were vulnerable to abduction, young girls were targets of those who treated children as a commodity, and tired, beaten and drained senior citizens were subjected to the most undignified treatment: Being cast aside, forgotten and unwanted.

In May 2005, the dormitories of Mercy Home opened and welcomed all: Men and women; Singhalese, Tamil and Muslim; Hindu, Buddhist or Christian. Before the calendar turned to another year, Mercy Home reflected a mosaic of Sri Lanka's sometimes troubled, always proud heritage. Some, including Valliyamma and her mother (who remained forever scarred by the slaughter of a 10-year-old boy), came to Mercy Home after a lifetime of suffering through poverty and despair.

For others, the facility offered a reminder of what they once knew, but which had since been taken away. Among the first residents was

Mr. Chandradasa, a gentle man whose inherent leadership qualities and quiet sense of wisdom – along with a notable resemblance to the legendary Indian leader – quickly earned him the nickname, "Mr. Gandhi." Born in Colombo in 1949, Chandradasa was the last of 10 children in a family headed by a postmaster father and an (obviously busy) housewife mother. By the late 1960s, unaware of a congenital heart defect, Chandradasa was studying at Colombo's St. Mary's College, hoping to follow in his father's footsteps with the postal service.

A career as a mail carrier was not in the plans, however, and Chandradasa worked a variety of jobs, including time with a British grain elevator. In 1983, when the start of the conflict made even the simplest business a struggling enterprise, his doctors advised him not to work, that his heart wouldn't last long doing physical labor.

He lost his job that year, and many friends, when the riots in Colombo included the looting and burning of a friend's store by Singhalese mobs. Lifelong friendships with Singhalese were strained, and Chandradasa joined the migration of many Tamils to northern regions of the country. The years that followed were unkind, and Chandradasa exhausted all means of assistance or employment. After a severe cardiac arrest in 1994, Chandradasa was released from the hospital to the streets, where he spent the next decade scratching out a meager, vagabond living, until a friend recommended him for residency in Mercy Home.

Chandradasa's story was hardly unique. As the war lingered on, the definitions of soldiers and enemies, targets and threats, became as blurred as the Sinhala-Tamil line. For a businessman named Nahayanan Karupaiya, born in 1923 near Kandy, his days as a young man included hotel management, running a clothing store and partnership in an auto transport business. Karupaiya was operating a small retail shop when, he said, "The ethnic problem" forced a relocation from Vavuniya for himself and his two children, a 24-year-old daughter and a son, 22.

Relocation couldn't escape the now ever-present threat of daily life

Division and unity: Some claim that post-tsunami tensions in Trincomalee began when a Singhalese political group placed a statue of Buddha on Tamil-owned property near the fish market (above). The statue was soon surrounded by concertina wire and the constant presence of security forces. (Below) Hiram Labrooy, Dr. Sathaharan Sundaralingam and Dr. Cheryl Huckins (standing, rear) helped train the growing staff of Mercy Home. (Photo courtesy Cheryl Huckins.)

in Sri Lanka. Both of his children, he said, were killed by members of the LTTE, despite the fact that Karupaiya and his family were Hindu Tamils. The murders, he said, began when his daughter attended a college course in the same class as a local police officer. Of similar ages and interests, the two were seen having a conversation away from the classroom.

Someone saw that, Karupaiya said, and rumors that his daughter was assisting the government's security forces – fueled by her turning down an offer to do broadcasting work for the Tigers – became accepted as truth.

"After that, they saw her talking with the police, and they shot her," Karupaiya said.

Likewise, his son had also turned down an offer to join the LTTE as a combatant, and was "made to disappear" in similar fashion. Both bodies were burned, Karupaiya said, and the downward spiral of his life, from merchant to nomad to vagrant, was coupled with the emptiness of never having been allowed a proper funeral for his children.

The riots of 1983 sparked retaliation attacks throughout the island; the war snowballed into far more clashes than just those between armed, uniform-wearing combatants. Kanahasabai Sevasegaram, a lifelong resident of Trincomalee born in 1920, enjoyed a large family in the eastern district that, one by one, were victims of poverty, illness, and war or civilian disturbances. Sevasegaram attended funerals for two wives – one to cancer another to illness – a brother in law and his own two brothers, who were killed in the war. A nephew was ambushed while on bicycle by civilians who were retaliating in response to rioting and looting in Colombo: A rope was thrown around his neck, yanking him off his bicycle before he was strangled to death. In 1983, two other nephews were dropped down a well to die a slow death.

Tragedy was as common as the farm labor Sevasegaram did as a young man, sweating it out in the fields surrounding Trincomalee, harvesting rice for three rupees a day. After the war started, business frequently stopped while people hid indoors, obeying the message found in the sight of a slain man and his six-year-old son whose bodies were placed in the middle of the road running from Trinco proper north to Nilaveli.

Before 1983, Sevasegaram had many Singhalese friends, but those bonds were tested after the trouble started. Suspicious looks replaced the easy smiles and casual pace of the northeastern district. At Mercy Home, where he was brought by a minister from an American mission, Sevasegaram said that new elders might, at first, be suspicious of the mixed environment. He himself was mistaken for Singhalese, due to his use of that language; that early miscommunication would later become the source of genuine laughs as the bonds of the community solidified with each new resident.

"We are like brothers from one family," he said, a feeling that extends to the modest crew on the grounds. The staff of Mercy Home grew to include the part-time efforts of U. Riyas, a young man who toiled a few hours a week for meager compensation – provided by a well-meaning Mercy Home manager who understood that Riyas and his family had their lives shattered by the tsunami.

Riyas was 20 years old and living in Jamalaiya when the disaster struck. That morning, with the memory of a family Christmas the day before, Riyas's father complained that the sea was getting rough, the air was troubled. They didn't believe him, dismissing it as a mild fever that laid him ill during the holiday. They humored him, and they helped drag the fishing boat to the sea shore to keep the old man happy.

While doing so, the reality of the problem soon became obvious. They gathered the family and ran upland to a road, where they were able to look down and see their home smashed by the pounding waves. They had brought nothing but the clothes on their back and their lives, and watched the waves sweep aside everything they had built as a family. Riyas, his father and brothers stayed with relatives, when possible, but what little extended family they had were not in any better position, and collectively they did what they could to survive. The government directed them to a local school, where crude huts were built on the playground before relocation was again made, this time to a "tsunami house," as Riyas called it.

The family struggled, and Riyas took part-time employment as a janitor at Trincomalee General Hospital and worked wherever extra money was available for basic cleaning chores. A charity organization eventually provided a boat engine to Riyas's father, shortly before a restriction on fishing was imposed by security forces. (A two-hour fishing expedition, when allowed, required hours of approval, verification and formalities to obtain permits.)

The tensions that covered the country beyond the Grace Care Center gates stayed outside; Mercy Home's mix of elders and staff formed a community with the girls of Grace Home. Chandradasa – "Mr. Gandhi" – lived up to his famous namesake with leadership qualities that inspired the growing population to feel pride of ownership and a sense of "home" that they thought would never again visit their lives. Chandradasa was among the early residents to seek out chores, and insist that everyone do what they were able to as payment for the blessing of a home.

Grace Care Center wasn't supposed to keep growing, but circumstance dictated opportunity, and a community was born. As the children of Grace Home reflect the future promise of what is possible for Sri Lanka; the elders of Mercy Home bore witness to a nation's troubled, violent past. Into Mercy Home came former shopkeepers, teachers, business owners and farmers alike, each victim to the longest-lasting effects of civil war – a nation too torn apart to support itself.

***

"I didn't plan any of these things, it just rolled out," Eric Parkinson said when the dream of Jeyanesan became the reality of Mercy Home.

Mercy Home wasn't the only element of Grace Care Center to open in the summer of 2005; the Vocational Training Center recognized the need for a dormitory to house some of its students, and 48 teenage girls took up residency on the blooming grounds. With only a hint of encouragement, routines were soon established that brought the Mercy Home elders into routine contact with the Grace Home and vocational training children.

"It made sense, and more and more the goal for Mercy Home was to help develop this sense of community," said Parkinson. "You've got kids who have no parents; you've got parents who have no kids. You've got parents who have a tremendous amount of wisdom; and children who are young and reckless. It's a natural."

(In what was becoming typical Grace Care Center synchronicity, Parkinson said that the property upon which Mercy Home sat, one of the seven total acres of Grace, wasn't included with the original purchase. The "land-locked" shape of the Mercy property was bordered by the six agreed-upon acres, and keeping it would have forced the property owner to establish a separate access road. With a shrug, the landowner simply added the parcel to the package.)

For the elders, the experiment worked both socially and, according to the doctors who planned the facility, medically.

"The mission always included the integration of the elders and the girls," said Gina Amalfitano. "It was slow to develop, but blossomed into something wonderful – it's almost a magical experience there. Inside those walls you can feel safe, at ease, and … maybe … at peace."

What surprised Amalfitano and Huckins was not the transformation of Grace Care Center, but the affect on elders they assumed would be less-than-active.

"The home is mostly populated with people who, although they have chronic conditions and need medical attention, they aren't bedridden," Amalfitano said. "Some of the elders are very spry, and some of them aren't all that old. The character of the place is more home-like than hospice like. It almost feels like a really nice camp for grown-ups who get to stay forever."

Valliyamma's mother, Ponnamma, for example, was unable to walk when first brought to the facility, but within a few months she began taking delicate, gentle strolls (typically accompanied by at least two eager children). The "miracle of Mercy Home," as VeAhavta visitors would call it, left people afraid to use the word, as it may have been too close to the truth.

The harmony of Mercy Home stood in stark contrast to the nation – and in Trincomalee itself – as tensions grew throughout the summer of 2005. The sense of common purpose and national unity inspired by the tsunami receded as the sounds of gunfire replaced the fading echoes of the ocean's roar. On Friday evening, Aug. 12, the country's 73-year-old Foreign Minister, Lakshman Kadirgamar, was assassinated on the rooftop of his Colombo home. Initially, police believed "one or two" snipers were responsible for the gunfire, which hit the Tamil minister several times in the head and chest while he relaxed on the deck of his apartment building.

Kadirgamar, who had served for 11 years as top administrator of Sri Lanka's foreign policy, openly encouraged the Tamil minority and Tigers to comply with the increasingly fragile cease-fire agreement. In published reports, the government claimed the motivation for the killing was fueled by the LTTE's refusal to accept the terms of the cease-fire; the Tigers, in turn, denied responsibility for the assassination, stating that an equal number of Singhalese supporters opposed the truce that Kadirgamar endorsed.

Earlier that same day, a well-known Tamil television broadcaster, Relangi Selvarajah, and her husband, politically active Sinnadurai Selvarajah, were gunned down at their Colombo house. Selvarajah was a news presenter for state television with the Sri Lanka Broadcasting Corporation; she also produced 'Idai Veenai," a current events program considered to be critical of the LTTE and supportive of the PLOTE, a political wing of Tamils who opposed the Tigers.

By Sunday, the English language newspapers stated as confirmed fact that the Kadirgamar killing was, "by a LTTE sniper." (Unlike most of the world's news agencies, the government-owned newspapers wasted no ink on words such as "alleged" or "suspected.") Kadirgamar's murder monopolized media attention, and there seemed little interest in conclusively identifying the assailant: The killing of the Selvarajah's remains unsolved, and was simply credited to the LTTE.

Tensions weren't limited to Colombo. In Trincomalee, the summer of 2005 began with the controversial placement of a Buddha statue on a piece of Tamil-owned property near the downtown fish market. The next day, the surrounding area was framed by concertina wire, sandbags and sentry posts, where a dozen soldiers joined the increasing number of security forces in Trincomalee.

Reportedly, a union of three-wheel taxi drivers placed the statue, although political groups including the pro-Singhalese JVP (Janatha Vimukthi Peramuna) have been credited with the dark-of-night planting. (This was the property seized by the JVP in February 2005 that launched the civil protest and hartal which sent Huckins, Amalfitano and the February team back to Colombo earlier than scheduled.) Rather than inspire the peace that Buddha would have wished for the troubled island, the statue drove a wedge between groups of scared, needy, angry citizens. One man who led a protest against the statue, Vanniasingam Vigneswaran, was shot to death; the bodies of five Tamil youths were found on the beach; and the largely Singhalese security forces found themselves under attack from suspected Tamil rebels. Frequent hartals, disturbances and religious and ethnic violence disturbed the peace in Trinco, where curfews were put in place that remained – off and on – for years as tensions elevated.

At Grace Care Center, shortly after the statue invited a division among residents, an ice cream social was held. The Grace Home girls played host to children from the Sivananda Thapovanam and Rawatha orphanages in Trincomalee. The 80, mostly Tamil, Hindu children from Thapovanam accepted the invitation, as did 20 Singhalese, Buddhist children from Rawatha: That facility's manager, Kamamaldeniye Pamgnabissa, a 36-year-old Buddhist monk, welcomed the opportunity to show his children that peace is possible between ethnic groups and religions.

(Concerning the statue, Pamgnabissa said it was a decision made on behalf of Singhalese politics, and not in accordance with the teachings of Buddha. "The way they placed that statue is not appropriate," he said. "The time period is not appropriate, and that place is not a suitable place." He also predicted that putting the statue in that place, at that time, would send the nation back to civil war. "Otherwise, people would have gone to peace," he said. "There was that possibility. Now, because of competition over who is having statues around, it wasn't hard to create war.")

The children spent a playful afternoon, holding hands, singing songs and finding quiet moments in the children's park, framed by an entry sign that reads, "True peace allows children the freedom to be children."

Death and fear dominated the daily lives of Sri Lankans as the tsunami faded to memory; the expectations of the cease-fire dwindled with each new act of war. In contrast, visitors to Grace Care Center marveled at the atmosphere that solidified even stronger against the growing tension.

"Mercy Home is a community now," said Cheryl Huckins. "It changed from a caretaker place to its own neighborhood. The residents helping out changed the dynamic and they learned to show respect for one another. This is their daily life," Huckins said of the violence that continued to scar a nation. At Mercy Home, the elders went from being patients to caretakers of their own lives. "Some sweep, some water plants, some pull weeds or collect coconuts. It brought the staff and residents together as equals, leading to mutual respect rather than a separation of those served and those who serve."

Before long, Hiram Labrooy, the all-around, go-to-guy of Grace Care Center, was appointed manager of Mercy Home. With a stern hand when needed and compassion always available, Labrooy was credited by VeAhavta's founding doctors with inspiring the sense of community at Mercy Home.

"We are working hard for it," Labrooy said. "We are trying to make our neighbors watch this place and the wonderful work they are doing without caring about race or religion. If that home can live like that, why can't our country live like that? Why can't the world live like that? It's a good example."

***

In spite of stories that easily could become legends, Mercy Home was not a miracle cure, and death would claim some of its family. Nearly 40 residents populated Mercy Home by the time a one-year anniversary was celebrated, a ceremony that included memories of six elders who had passed away since coming to the home.

Those who helped plan the facility believed they had taken into consideration the proper arrangements for dealing with an elder's death. The written policy called for the deceased to be taken for burial preparations, typically expected to be a church, which would tend to the funeral arrangements.

When an elder passed away after having been taken to Trincomalee General Hospital, Cheryl Huckins received a late-night, anguished call from Labrooy.

"The elders insisted that the body be brought back to Grace," Huckins said; they wanted to hold their own memorial service for someone who had become part of their family before the body was taken elsewhere. Labrooy felt duty-bound to follow the policy, but compelled to satisfy such a determined wish on the part of his residents. (Huckins quickly made, "Clearly the right decision," when she told Labrooy to respect and honor the wishes of the community. The elder was brought back to the seven-acre compound for the first of many ceremonies that were sad, yet affirming in their dignity.

By the time Mr. Chandradasa – "Mr. Gandhi" – passed away in October 2006, it was clear that, to the elders, a peaceful, dignified death was the final gift that Mercy Home bestowed upon their lives.

In October, Chandradasa developed a blood clot, which raised heightened concerns given "Mr. Gandhi's" history of heart trouble. He was taken to Colombo, where further complications and conditions were discovered. Soon, the decision was made to amputate part of his left leg. The surgery seemed a success, although complications continued.

In his final days, Chandradasa had a near-constant bedside companion, Diane McLaughlin, who first visited Grace Care Center in August 2005 and returned, in December, to begin what would be a one-year stay as in-residence manager of the growing compound. The days spent with Chandradasa were filled with memories, a little crying, and a lot of laughter, McLaughlin said.

"I was there until shortly before he died," McLaughlin said. "We were enjoying one another's company to the fullest: Still laughing, some tears, and everything in between."

Chandradasa was very much at peace in his final days, McLaughlin said. "He put up the best fight he had in him, and held his head high, treating everyone with dignity, respect and kindness. Even in the worst of times, he was gentle with his words and forgiving with his heart."

Chandradasa told McLaughlin that the miracle of Mercy Home was not a renewed sense of vitality in tired old hearts, but of a simple state of existence that many of them had forgotten.

"They're all in the same boat," McLaughlin said. "No matter what religion or ethnic background, they are thankful for the opportunity to live their remaining days in peace."

At Mercy Home they found what they thought was forever gone, the absence of the daily fear that had been their lives for decades. Chandradasa died, he said, no longer afraid for his life.

Encounters
Praying for Friends

It's always a good day when you can make several girls burst into fits of giggles and smiles. Burning the soles of your feet is a small price to pay.

On a Sunday afternoon in early 2006, I joined a busload of Grace Home girls for a visit to Tiru Koneswaram, a Hindu temple on a cliff overlooking Trincomalee's harbor. Getting to the temple required two things: A 100-meter walk up a steep, paved incline; and the tradition of removing footwear before entering the sacred grounds.

A "field trip" with dozens of active children is, by nature, a hectic, confusing adventure, and I didn't give much thought to removing my sandals at the entrance before starting the climb to Koneswaram.

About 10, maybe 12 steps up the hill, I realized the pavement was pretty hot: It was early afternoon; the sun had been up for seven, eight hours; and the day's temperatures topped 100-degrees Fahrenheit. The children's feet were calloused enough for them to carry on without interference.

Mine, of course, were not.

"Wow," I believe I said. "Oh, boy." The stone path was more than just a "little hot." Picking one foot up did nothing to help the other, no matter how rapidly I began dancing in place.

That's what started the girls giggling.

"Pretty funny, huh?" I asked, to the general agreement of those walking with me. "Let's head over to that shady spot, shall we?"

Stopping briefly under a tree, I was afraid to look down, certain I would see smoke curling out from the soles of my feet. I negotiated a zig-zag course that balanced shaded portions of the path with the roasting, searing, naked-to-the-sun pavement. I took a deep breath, assured the giggling girls that I was okay, and the journey continued.

No question, though, it was worth it. Koneswaram, the "Temple of a Thousand Columns," probably had as many names over the years as it held legends and myths. Among its designations, including "The Sacred Hill of the Three Temples" and the "Thousand Pillared Mandapam," the name "Kona Malai" may be the oldest, driven from the same phrase – "tiru-kona-malai" that became "Trincomalee" (the Sacred Hill of the Lord). In its current form, Koneswaram was built shortly after the Dutch destroyed its predecessor on the same ground in 1624. (Pieces from the original temple, statues of Ganesha and other Hindu figures, were discovered in the 1950s in a cave at the foot of the cliff.) Religion and military strategy have sought the cliff – the crest of which is called Swami Rock – for devotional or strategic purposes dating back to King Panduvasdeva, said to have claimed the imposing point in the 5th Century BC.

Along with the shrine and prayer stations, Swami Rock is home to a granite pillar of mythical origin. A popular legend is that a Dutch father built the monument in memory of his daughter, who leaped to the sea in passionate suicide after being abandoned by a sailor lover. (Other historians found records of the same woman marrying later in life, and instead claim that the pillar was a form of lighthouse to warn sailors of the pending rocks they would encounter.)

No matter the story, Koneswaram holds a history of worship and belief, of treasures claimed or cast aside by one civilization to be fought over by distant descendants. Time in Sri Lanka (the latest in a series of names for the island) is measured by centuries as it is elsewhere in years or decades.

We stayed at Koneswaram for about an hour. The girls of the Hindu faith went through their customary prayers; visitors marveled at the intricate carvings and sincerity of the rituals. Two of the Grace children walked me by the hand to a box perched atop a stand. A string from my shirt was gently taken and tied to the prayer box; their little heads bowed in silent wishes for my well-being.

In pairs and small groups, we walked the triangular-shaped grounds, taking in the views of the sea, of the harbor and of Trinco's shoreline. At the most elevated spot in Trincomalee, a cool wind filled the silence in harmony with the sounds of the ocean. For centuries, the promise of paradise had lured

Statues and legends: The "Temple of a Thousand Columns," Tiru
Koneswaram, has long stood watch from a cliff overlooking Trincomalee.
The current temple was rebuilt after its predecessor was razed by the Dutch
in the early 1600s; the location has been used for worship – or war – since
the 5th Century BC.

Names for the temple atop Swami Rock (above) included "Tiru Kona-Malee," derived from the same phrase that became "Trincomalee." (Below) The author enjoyed a cliff-top view with "the baby," Ramesh Dachayani, and was able to point out the distant Grace Care Center during a visit to the temple in February 2006. (Photo by Erin Whaley.)

so many to that very spot; others, on occasion, have threatened to poison the peace it offered.

We walked (gently) back to the entrance, which bordered Fort Frederick, a military outpost with its own history. There was more than the usual number of soldiers in Trinco in recent weeks, and more determined troops were a common, daily part of the girls' landscape. (A few days earlier I was running an errand with Hiram Labrooy, who steered a van through the narrow, congested streets of Trinco's market district. At a fork in the road, we were cut off by a military flatbed truck, its cargo area covered by canvas to keep the sun off the soldiers inside – eight troops with black masks worn under their steel pot helmets, covering all but the young eyes of Special Task Force soldiers. The masks were worn, Labrooy explained in simple, direct words, "to scare people.") Additional checkpoints established the previous month would remain in place and manned; soldiers walking patrol on the rooftops of the market district were common sights.

The youngest of the Grace children, perhaps possessing the blissful ignorance of youth, may assume that everyone in the world lives as they do, unaware of the extreme nature of their situation. At Koneswaram, these same children said a prayer for me. It was their custom to pray for the well being of others more than to seek spiritual favors for selfish pursuit. Prayer requires little translation to understand the intent, whether offered in a Buddhist shrine, a Hindu Temple (of stubborn longevity and heritage unknown in most of the world), a Muslim mosque or the church at Grace Care Center. Stripped of dogma and free of agenda, these are simple prayers, really: That their friends would be happy, and not get hurt.

We left the temple grounds and began the short drive back to the orphanage. The beach near Koneswaram was well populated with soldiers.

The little ones may not have known that their futures were threatened more than most, but the older girls knew that not everyone lived this way, in a war that didn't spare teenagers from being casualties. Just a few weeks earlier, five boys their own age had been killed not far from the temple grounds.

"This was in an area with a lot of young people.
If they were killed here, it could happen
to anyone, anywhere."
— Dr. Sathaharan Sundarlingam

Chapter 7

'The Little Ones are Getting Scared'

After the first day back in class, students from Trincomalee's schools relaxed near the beach. It was January 2; a new year offered an excuse to wonder if this would be the time of peace, or would history instead record a return to war.

Seven boys, classmates and friends from Sri Koneswara Hindu and St. Joseph's colleges, spent a few minutes together in the early evening. Koneswara welcomed some of Trinco's brightest young men; the 100-plus year old school (established in 1897 by Hindu luminaries) boasted from among its 2,000 students the highest number of boys in the district to qualify for university studies. Among the last to join the group was Shanmugarajah Sajendran, who first went from his day's science and engineering courses to offer "pooja," an evening prayer at the historic Hindu temple, Tiru Koneswaram.

The prospects for peace or university studies were, perhaps, among Sajendran's thoughts, but not exclusively: A cousin recalled him as a good-looking young man, "Full of humor" and – much to his family's ongoing amusement – popular with the girls. He should study more and think of girls less, his family gently warned, although they were justifiably proud when Sajendran's grades frequently placed him near the top of his class.

They were an ambitious group: One was a local champion at chess, another held skills at table tennis that were so valued he frequently gave lessons; he included among his students members of the local police force who were trying to improve their game.

At the Pinnewala elephant orphanage, near the central resort town of
Kandy, Diane McLaughlin gets to know one of the larger members of the
animal community. Tourist destinations such as Pinnewala – among the
largest sanctuaries in the world dedicated to saving elephants abandoned by
their herds – were rare moments for McLaughlin during her tenure as in-
residence manager of Grace Care Center.

It was their first time together since before the holidays, and talk of current events included recent threats to the cease-fire. It was a frequent topic in Trinco, clearly of interest to the nation's young men. A few days earlier, 2005 ended with a security-driven sweep in the country's capital during which 920 mostly Hindu Tamils were arrested in Colombo. Of those taken into custody, only five men were charged as being members of the LTTE. The search was conducted by 2,400 police officers, supported by 2,000 soldiers, sailors and air force personnel, who systematically blocked off congested streets and went door-to-door in pursuit of suspects.

There were other stories to tell, some even closer to Trincomalee. The boys brought each other up-to-date on family and mutual acquaintances seen over the holidays. Sajendran stopped for a visit with his friends after descending the hill from Koneswaram, walking from the temple grounds and entering the edge of the market district. Not far from the sandbagged bunkers at the entrance to Fort Frederick, a small herd of white-patched deer grazed on a patch of grass surrounding a traffic circle.

Sajendran walked past the checkpoint staffed by more than the usual number of troops. At the beach, he spent a few moments with his friends, just one small group among dozens; hundreds of people enjoyed the cool breeze that floated off the bay.

Many of them were witnesses to what happened next, when a grenade exploded, shots were fired, and five students were killed.

**

When asked what she missed most about America, Diane McLaughlin's memories might seem modest to some, but they were priceless to her: A coffee shop, book store or, in particular, a neighborhood bar, a place to unwind with friends, listen to music and shoot some pool. A simple memory that, in some ways, summarized what "back home" and "family" meant to her.

Nostalgia would have to wait, however; McLaughlin's days were quickly filled with the next crisis to be addressed. December 2005 was a far cry from being an ideal time for McLaughlin to take up residency in Trincomalee and assume responsibility for up to 100 girls; a dozen elders (with more arriving weekly); the Vocational Training and Day Care programs; and staff of more than a dozen.

Before making her first trip to Sri Lanka in August 2005, McLaughlin was more familiar with America's vast heartland than with the geography of southern Asia.

"I didn't even know where Sri Lanka was," she admitted. "I think I knew it was below India, the little tear-drop shaped place. That's what I remembered from history class." She may have heard occasional reports about a war (one among many) on the other side of the planet, but McLaughlin had more pressing, day-to-day concerns as service coordinator and cottage manager for Catholic Charities Services in Cleveland, Ohio. Dealing with at-risk, often abused and vulnerable city kids was, by then, second nature to McLaughlin, who previously spent three years as program manager for the Children's Crisis Center in Helena, Montana, and before that as a case manager with the Jesuit Volunteer Corps.

The tsunami made Sri Lanka a more familiar place on the world's current map, and in March, 2005 McLaughlin met Dr. Naresh Gunaratnam, a colleague of McLaughlin's brother in Ann Arbor, Michigan, who told her about a struggling orphanage in northeast Sri Lanka.

The timing was right: McLaughlin needed a change, a transition from the emotionally exhaustive work she did in Cleveland; Gunaratnam knew of a Michigan-based team preparing for a late-summer trip to Grace Care Center, where McLaughlin's social skills could help assess the needs of the bustling orphanage.

McLaughlin made her first trip in August, and felt a connection that begged for further exploration. It was an expansive period for VeAhavta, ignited by a post-tsunami increase in funds and interest. During an October 2005 meeting in Michigan, VeAhavta President Eric Parkinson announced that he was taking a one-year sabbatical from his California law practice to dedicate his full attention to the

Fallen friends: Walls lining the streets of Trincomalee held frequent tributes (above) to five students – Shanmugarajah Sajendran, Lohitharaja Rohan, Thangathurai Sivanantha, Yogarajah Hemachandran and Manoharan Rajihar – who were killed on January 2, 2006. (Below) The park areas near the harbor were a common meeting place for students from nearby universities and colleges. A deer relaxes in the shade where the five boys were killed a month earlier.

non-profit organization he established and its principal cause, Grace Care Center.

At that same meeting, McLaughlin told the group of her next career plan: To spend one year (at least) as in-residence manager of the facility. McLaughlin and Parkinson traveled to Trinco in November for a first-hand look at what might be possible; by December she was installed as the manager of Grace Care Center. Her "home" would be a small room on the orphanage property, initially decorated with pictures of family and friends but soon sharing wall space with wax paintings of pole fishermen. Regardless of the dimensions of her quarters (or loss of the familiar ritual of a friendly game of pool), McLaughlin quickly felt as if she were, in fact, "home."

"This is where I'm supposed to be," McLaughlin said, something she understood practically from the moment she arrived. McLaughlin's professional experience told her that the needs of the children were too deep to be quickly, or easily, resolved. Understanding the trauma that had shaped the lives of these children would take time – a schedule that couldn't even begin until a basic trust was developed.

"You can't get to the root of these issues in one week or even three months," McLaughlin said. "There's so much more involved when you're asking someone to open up and peel the layers that they've built up oh-so-well. Their skin is thicker than anything."

At Grace, McLaughlin saw the opportunity to both serve and to see the results of that service up close and personal, with hands-on work and an eyewitness view of the outcome. The idea of making such a dramatic change in her life was born during her trip in August, contemplated through September and, after visiting the facility with Parkinson in November, confirmed by the end of the year.

She didn't go in blindly, though, nor unaware of the additional risks and problems beyond the considerable amount created with relocation, the loss of daily contact with family and friends, and a career path in her mid-30s that would be difficult to put back on track when (if) she left Grace Care Center.

A town on alert: Security forces became increasingly common sights in Trinco after late 2005. Tensions that began when the Buddha statue was placed on Tamil-owned land escalated dramatically after the deaths of five students, and continued climbing as the cease-fire's impact diminished. Each passing incident brought the nation closer to a return to all-out, open warfare involving the government, the LTTE and several paramilitary groups aligned to one side or the other.

Those thoughts were for another day; the immediacy of Sri Lanka's problems became more evident with each passing month. In November, polling places throughout the country were well-staffed with AK-47-toting police and security forces for the country's presidential election. The support from the ruling JVP party that brought President Chandrika Kumaratunga to office in April 2004 abandoned her in mid-2005 over, in part, a dispute about the distribution of tsunami relief supplies. Then-prime minister Mahinda Rajapakse, with the support of the Singhalese United People's Freedom Alliance party, narrowly (with just over 50 percent of the vote) defeated Ranil Wickremesinghe, the opposition leader responsible for brokering the 2002 ceasefire agreement. Wickremesinghe was viewed by many as being conciliatory to the Tamil Tigers, while Rajapakse's platform maintained a tough stance against the LTTE, with "Eelam" not an option and favoring a "national economy" that discouraged private industry. (The news caused further uncertainty about Sri Lanka's place on the international stock market, already vulnerable to tsunami fears and speculation.)

The November 2005 election was a confusing campaign to report, and international monitors wondered about the motives behind the politics. Pro-Tiger organizations distributed leaflets urging Tamil citizens in the north to boycott the election; one Tamil fisherman told a reporter of being prevented from casting his ballot by soldiers. "I tried to vote, but they hit me on the head," he said. Polls were not open in Jaffna; civil protests and roads with burning-tire blockades were common sights. When Rajapakse, a 59-year-old, staunchly anti-Tamil independence politician was confirmed as the nation's next president, the victory was said to have been assisted by the very rebels he opposed.

The grace period of peace following the tsunami was quickly fading. As the one-year anniversary of the disaster approached, the New York Times reported: "A fresh wave of political violence is sweeping across eastern Sri Lanka. Armed factions vie for supremacy, assassinations and abductions go on in broad daylight, and parents squirrel away their children for fear they will be conscripted into battle."

The first month of the Rajapakse administration included frequent clashes between Tigers and government troops. "Fears of a return to civil war" was a phrase used by many news agencies. On Christmas morning, Parliamentarian Joseph Pararajasingaham was gunned down while attending midnight mass at St. Mary's Cathedral in Batticaloa; in Jaffna, five civilians, including a woman, were shot dead as they returned from church; two other civilians were killed in Batticaloa's Amman Hindu Temple.

The violence was blamed on the LTTE. American officials, including Sen. Richard Lugar of the Foreign Relations Committee, told the Sri Lankan government they could count on U.S. support. Secretary of State Condoleezza Rice expressed admiration for what she called Sri Lanka's, "Restraint in the face of the Tamil Tigers' provocations," and used the word "terrorism" in reference to the rebel group.

Echoes of the holiday violence were heard – and repeated – in Trinco. On Christmas Day, two tuk-tuk drivers accepted fares going from the market district; their bodies were found at 4 Milepost on a stretch of narrow road north of Grace Care Center that winds through barren, seaside fields. On Dec. 27 in Sangaman, three miles from Trincomalee town, a soldier on leave was killed in his home by a grenade.

Away from her family, her friends and her life, Diane McLaughlin spent a cautious Christmas with the children, elders and staff of Grace Care Center – friends she made in August that quickly became "family" in every possible definition – clinging to what was now her life, too. McLaughlin ended 2005 by starting what was supposed to be a one-year term of service. Strategies designed in the comfort of a conference room in Michigan gave way to the realities of a volatile situation.

"You have to change your game plan," McLaughlin said. "If the needs of the people here are truly your mission, you don't stick with whatever your own, personal agenda was. You change and adapt when you see what's needed."

***

Five boys were killed: Shanmugarajah Sajendran and his companions, Lohitharaja Rohan, Thangathurai Sivanantha, Yogarajah Hemachandran and Manoharan Rajihar, pronounced dead upon arrival at Trincomalee General Hospital on Jan. 2. How they died, and what the world would be told, made for "A day of big drama" at Trinco General, according to senior medical office Dr. Sathaharan Sundaralingam.

"Satha," as he was known to the residents of Mercy Home and friends of Grace Care Center, was familiar with the results of war, both as a physician and during his days as a student. His university studies in Jaffna in the early 1990s were interrupted twice when explosions destroyed the school.

Satha's weekly visits to patients at Mercy Home was born from a relationship that began in early 2005, when VeAhavta's first post-tsunami group investigated a partnership between Trinco General and St. Joseph Mercy Hospital in Ann Arbor. From advisor and consultant, Satha quickly became a familiar face at Mercy Home following its May 2005 opening, holding clinic once a week that he added to his 60-plus hours logged at the Trinco General. He was in attendance when five fatally injured young men were brought to the hospital.

What angered Satha most – the physician's darkest nightmare – was the belief that two of the boys could have been saved, had they been taken to the hospital sooner. Seven boys were brought to the morgue (not the emergency room); two had survived their injuries and would be treated. The seven did not arrive until nearly an hour after the shootings, which took place just a few kilometers from the hospital. Satha speculated that two of the fatalities were preventable with earlier medical attention.

The story would take weeks to clarify, months to resolve, to little satisfaction. The earliest statements made through official channels said the boys were handling a grenade and it detonated; another story was that the students were planning to use the device against security forces.

The grenade, it was finally admitted, did not belong to Sajendran and his friends, but was instead thrown in their general direction from a passing tuk-tuk, a drive-by grenading on the beach of Dutch Bay. After the explosion, Sajendran and his friends saw Navy troops and Special Task Force personnel from nearby Fort Frederick hurry to encircle the area. Aware of the danger, the boys tried to leave. One, Manoharan Rajihar, used his cell phone to call his father, a respected doctor, who hurried to the beach but was stopped at a checkpoint. The surrounding area had been blocked off by military and police.

Sajendran and his friends, now "guilty" of trying to get away from security forces, were herded by soldiers into a small circle on a grassy slope near a traffic circle. A cargo truck pulled alongside, and two of the boys were loaded into the back. Two were seen being made to kneel, and were shot in the back of the head (in the words of too many witnesses to discount), "execution style." More gunshots were heard from near the truck before it left the area.

The "big drama" Satha witnessed at Trinco General included attempts to falsify the report on cause of death. Dr. Gamini Gunatunga, a Sinhalese physician who performed the post-mortem examination, would not confirm the military's assertion (already released by the government to news agencies) that the boys were killed by a grenade.

"They tried to manipulate the medical officer who did the post mortem," said Satha, who described a swarm of soldiers inside the hospital and a growing mob outside (estimated at 300 villagers) demanding answers. "He was very honest. He said, 'I can't do that,'" when asked to confirm the grenade as the source of the fatal injuries. (Gunatunga's courageous statement was confirmed when photographs of the fatal injuries appeared in Tamil publications, clearly proving gunshot wounds as the cause of death.)

Beyond the tensions in the hospital, the community fell under the cloud of Satha's worst nightmares, fears that began when he first heard the news of the killings. The war had come to town, he thought, and it would not remain as a single incident. The random nature of the deaths shattered any sense of safety that might have still existed.

"This was in an area with a lot of young people," Satha said. "If someone can just come and shoot you like that, you were worried about going outside. If they were killed here, it could happen to anyone, anywhere."

***

Diane McLaughlin sent frequent e-mails to her friends in America, asking that, if nothing else, some prayers be sent her way, a request made on behalf of the 80-plus girls she protected.

"Some of the little ones are getting scared," McLaughlin wrote. "That happens often."

January rolled on in a wave of violence that echoed in and around Trinco and throughout Sri Lanka. On Jan. 7, a fishing boat filled with explosives rammed a Sri Lankan navy vessel, killing 13 sailors. The Sea Tigers – the maritime branch of the LTTE – took out the 24-foot ship in what could be called a suicide boat attack. Two of the 15 sailors on board survived, and were found clinging to wreckage the next morning. (Trinco's harbor was no stranger to war on the sea: When the Japanese navy attempted to take control of the area during World War II, a group of Tamil fishermen managed to sink a Japanese battleship, now a fixture on the ocean floor for scuba divers to tour.)

Again, the shops, schools and town of Trincomalee were closed. A fishing ban – the first in what would become an ongoing series – was put into effect, nullifying the fruitful waters that drove Trinco's economy. Explosions close enough to be heard inside the walls of Grace Care Center became a daily reality. McLaughlin told the younger girls that the grenades and gunfire sounds were just people still celebrating New Year's. The older, sadly wiser girls half-heartedly supported this fairy tale for the benefit of the smaller children. No one was fooling anyone: The kids knew what war sounds like.

For the second time in a week, Sri Lankan officials said a full investigation would be launched. Legal paperwork mounted alongside casualties: In December 2005, nearly 50 police and troops were killed, which was reported as the deadliest month yet since the cease fire. The first two weeks of 2006 topped that number, and more than 200 deaths would be reported in January, fatalities that included an equal mix of combatant and civilian. A Navy bus was ambushed on the outskirts of Trinco when a bicycle with a landmine strapped to it rammed the vehicle while ambushing Tigers opened fire and wounded seven security troops. In Batticaloa, a bomb was set off outside of the offices of the truce-brokering Sri Lanka Monitoring Mission, which on Jan. 18 indefinitely suspended its efforts in Trinco. Yet another journalist, Subramaniyam Sugirdharajan of the Tamil newspaper "Sudaroli," was gunned down on Jan. 24, the day after publishing a report on abuses committed by Tamil political organizations. (The same newspaper was targeted in August 2005 when a grenade attack took out its printing press in Colombo.) Headlines routinely described the ceasefire as "threatened," and that the northern and eastern districts were heading back to "all-out war."

At the end of the first week of January, a Saturday night talent show was held at Grace Care Center, during which the girls entertained the staff and elders with dances, songs, poems and, in classic show-must-go-on tradition, a comedy routine directed by the Tiger-trained Sundari, who remained determined to study books and not take up arms.

An hour after the show, an explosion was heard from the access road. The grenade blast was followed by a burst of gunfire; seven, maybe eight rounds were fired well within hearing range of the orphanage, sending a group of girls who had been playing near the gate screaming for their lives.

Each day brought new concerns, responsibilities, and challenges to overcome. Makeshift classroom lessons were given on the orphanage grounds. When travel was permitted, McLaughlin and a crew of Grace staff rounded up supplies and delivered any surplus they could spare to nearby orphanages and care facilities that she had formed relationships with. She recorded brief entries on a desk calendar for later reference: "Two shot today," "Explosions heard down the road," "Five killed."

It became harder for McLaughlin to think of the violence as remote, or disconnected; yet the seven acres of serenity allowed that illusion. Something about the spirit of the place, the girls, encouraged such thoughts.

"I am sheltered in this bubble called Grace," McLaughlin said. "By 'sheltered' I mean 'safe'." Somehow, McLaughlin was certain; no one would harm her, the staff or, "My babies," the children of Grace Care Center.

What scared the children more than the actual sounds of war was the potential loss of McLaughlin. Sundari, explaining the somber mood of the girls, told her of their main concern: "You go to America," she said, "And the Grace girls cry and cry."

McLaughlin did her best to assure them, words promising what only action could deliver: "I am not going back to America," McLaughlin told the people of Grace. "I am staying right here with all of you."

Others were afraid that the renewed conflict and ongoing hartals would prevent a planned February visit by VeAhavta visitors. Privately, McLaughlin wondered what would be left of Trinco if visitors did come. Her concerns extended beyond the walls of Grace, where the children, elders and skeleton staff were seemingly locked in for the foreseeable future. For extended periods of time, there was an eerie silence past the gate, "No noise from the roads," McLaughlin said. "No fishermen going in or out. The only people moving around are the armed forces."

The hartal kept the stores closed for days on end; the Methodist Girls College was not expected to open again until the end of the month. The cabinets and food pantry at Grace Care Center were getting bare, as the shops of Trinco were closed for more than a week. Grace was better equipped than most to handle a prolonged period without supplies, McLaughlin knew, but she worried about the other orphanages in the area, and about the vulnerable people next door in Alles Gardens, the informal camp of families displaced by the conflict or the tsunami.

On Jan. 16, the hartal was lifted, and the markets again opened to feed and supply a community. The next day, on Jan. 17, a crude, home-made claymore mine of ball bearings and gunpowder was detonated in a small general store at the entrance road to Grace Care Center. Up to a dozen soldiers were injured in the blast, which took the lives of two civilian shopkeepers. Again, the stores were closed, and during the hartal that followed, Grace Care Center temporarily increased its population with the families from Alles Gardens, seeking refuge (again) inside the relative peace of the orphanage.

The girls played cricket, did their chores and flew kites with the elders of Mercy Home. They grew alarmed when they reported to McLaughlin a sight they had not previously seen: "Men with guns" took control of the beach.

During her first visit in August, McLaughlin and her traveling companions were able to convince the girls to again play in the ocean after the tsunami inspired fears that kept them from splashing in its waves for months. A year later, they would, again, be afraid to play in their own backyard.

***

An investigation was, as promised conducted; the final account of the killings remained inconclusive. The boys came from families with enough means to force the matter – albeit at their own risk – to be heard in court. The story was closely watched both in country and internationally; coming on the heels of the tsunami's one-year anniversary and the Christmas morning killings in Batticaloa and Jaffna, more worldly attentions were, briefly, paid to Sri Lanka.

The innocence of the victims, in spite of initial government reports, was confirmed, and no evidence was found that the boys had any involvement with the rebels.

"The people who died have proven to be university students," said V. Yogeswaran, whose legal knowledge as an attorney was guided by the moral compass of his work as a Jesuit priest. "That is one reason this blew up to greater proportions."

Yogeswaran attended the two days' worth of testimony that began on March 13 before the Presidential Commission Investigating Serious Violations of Human Rights, held in Trincomalee Magistrate Court. Witnesses included Dr. Kasipillai Manoharan, whose son Rajihar was among the victims. His statement was given via video conference from another country.

(Manoharan's claims that he was harassed and threatened were not the only ones that came from relatives of the victims who insisted they would speak their minds. Manoharan said the tactics ranged from physical threats by security forces to a call from a cabinet minister, who offered a house in Colombo and other compensations if he would not press the matter.)

"I can still hear my son's voice," Manoharan testified; "Screaming for his life while he was being executed."

At the time of the hearings, Yogeswaran was working out of a Jesuit academy in Trincomalee while trying to establish a Center for the Promotion and Protection of Human Rights. The testimony he heard frustrated (if not insulted) him; these were simply the latest in a series of murders in the northeast, and in spite of the public nature of the attacks, witnesses were kept far enough away from the area to confirm too much.

No matter how passionate the words of grieving fathers, Yogeswaran said that justice was unlikely to be served. It would have been difficult to determine which branch of security forces were involved, let alone assign the fatal bullets to the specific rifles of individuals – especially if the assailants wore unmarked uniforms and black masks. Yogeswaran said there were more Navy personnel in the area, but that Special Task Force troops were also a growing presence in Trincomalee.

The identities might remain unknown, but Yogeswaran said the testimony confirmed that those who pulled the triggers did so with official support.

"Whoever it was, the military knew," Yogeswaran said. "They had the road blocks, they knew who was coming. The presumption is that it was someone known to the military, or someone who was part of the military. It was not done without the military having knowledge of it."

The deaths of the five students were listed among the 16 most serious allegations of human rights abuses that took place in 2006, and in September President Mahinda Rajapakse appointed a special Commission of Inquiry to study these charges. By early 2007, the committee had yet to become operational.

***

Diane McLaughlin followed through on her promise to greet the February VeAhavta visitors, "Like you've never been greeted before." The small team, including a Michigan doctor and teacher who had been to the orphanage the previous year, spent a pleasant 10 days with old friends.

In honor of their visitors, the children again staged a talent show, with songs that didn't require translation to be enjoyed, enthusiastic dancing, and, as always, comedy routines. The performance concluded with a poem for peace read by Ushna Kristhamoothry, who also guided a group of singers for an English version of "This Land is Your Land." Rewritten lyrics cited the need to find unity between "Capital Colombo" with "Trincomalee," in place of the link Woody Guthrie made from California to the New York highlands.

In late February, the first round of a new series of truce negotiations was held in Geneva between the government and the LTTE, a session that ended inconclusively but with the promise to curtail paramilitary activities and to meet again in April. The violence of early 2006 settled, briefly; each sunset that ended another day without death tempted people to, again, believe that peace might be possible.

Classes at Methodist Girls College resumed, and each morning McLaughlin waved goodbye to a school bus crowded with what she called, "My babies." It was a rough month, January, but McLaughlin remembered the first day when the hartal was lifted, and she was free to shop for supplies. She passed a Sri Lankan friend as people casually went about their business, grateful for the simple routine of taking care of their families and walking freely in their community, their home.

"The stores are laughing again," McLaughlin was told, with a smile. The broken-English declaration simply defined what 'laughing' can be: Free to be open, to be happy. The stores were laughing, and the people enjoyed the sounds.

"That was a great day," McLaughlin said. "I pray it continues."

No, Father, the Beatles Broke Up

"You gotta meet this guy," Naresh Gunaratnam said, with typical (usually justified) excitement. "He's amazing. He's been here about 50 years."

The phrase "small world" just isn't strong enough for connections like this. In an accidental encounter, the Sri Lankan-born Gunaratnam met Father Lloyd Anthony Lorio, an American priest from New Orleans, at the Trincomalee offices of the United States Agency for International Development. That evening, Lorio joined our post-tsunami volunteer team for dinner at Grace Care Center, the first meeting of what would become an ongoing partnership and relationship between the orphanage and the Jesuit Academy managed by Lorio. (Before that, Lorio was unfamiliar with the children's home not far down the road from his operation.)

There was a lot to learn from this man, both for the future of Trinco and from the journey that had been his life. In 1951, while in his early 20s, Lorio answered the call to serve as one of a handful of American Jesuits from the Louisiana province at their Ceylon mission. Lorio spent five weeks traveling by boat from America. (Put in perspective, our "grueling" two-day, door-to-door trip suddenly paled in comparison.) Fortunately, his initial assignment in Batticaloa could be reached by train; rail was not an option for the priests who arrived just a few years earlier, when going from Colombo to the northeast required a slow boat ride around the southern coast.

Lorio's was not, however, a story of sacrificing convenience for a life of hardship. From his perspective, it was just the opposite: He left a nation on the verge of becoming, in his estimation, prisoners to television and air conditioning, a society that placed barriers and put distance between neighbors, friends and communities; the post-World War II population in America preferred privacy fences to front porches; city populations declined as sprawling suburbs sought further separation.

Father Lloyd Anthony Lorio, a Jesuit priest from New Orleans, first moved to Ceylon in 1951 at the request of the Louisiana Parish. With rare exception, he has remained in Sri Lanka since, teaching students in southern port towns, Batticaloa and Trinco. Lorio's calling included knowing the most efficient escape route for the children under his watch, typically featuring a peaceful mix of Sri Lankan students.

Lorio's initial impression of Sri Lanka, he said, was of a nation and people able to live together in peace. For the next half a century, Lorio watched that security turn deadly; he grew from a young man to, at the turn of the 21ˢᵗ Century, a man approaching 80 with a balding pate and shoulders stooped from hardships and suffering unimaginable in America.

From Lorio's vantage point on a harbor-skirting road, the Asian tsunami must have seemed the realization of a Biblical disaster. Lorio spent the days after the tragedy puttering around the villages on a scooter, consoling those who lost everything, including hope for any kind of future. Self-inflicted death rates in Sri Lanka had always been on the high end of the international scale, and Lorio talked to many potential suicides in the wake of the tsunami. Success was, as always, balanced with sad reality.

As a relationship between Grace Care Center and Father Lorio's academy grew, visitors continued to learn more about the man, his hopes and his mission. In the months and years after the tsunami, the prayers of a gentle old priest (whom the women of VeAhavta routinely described using the words "cute," "cuddly" or "adorable") were often challenged. He grew discouraged, and even the prospects of a promising project occasionally overwhelmed his ability to believe in success.

"Remember, Father," I searched for words of optimism. "'There's nothing you can do that can't be done,'" A simple, lightweight (yet admirable) piece of philosophy offered against a near-hopeless situation.

Lorio smiled in appreciation for the message; I explained the source: John Lennon's lyrics from The Beatles' "All You Need is Love."

"Ahh," Lorio said, acknowledging that he had heard of the group. "They're not together any more, are they?"

"No, Father," I smiled, nodded, and confirmed the "news" to him, 30-plus years after the fact. "The Beatles broke up."

A beautiful man, Father Lorio, possessing both innocence and the sad wisdom learned only through harsh experience. He found it difficult to believe in good things that might happen, but was well aware that bad things could, and probably would take place. If it challenged his beliefs, he wouldn't admit it. His faith was his life.

Places of peace: The Jesuit Academy overseen by Lorio (above) continues to work for the future education of northeast Sri Lanka's children, with an emphasis on computer and English skills. In times of conflict, compounds such as an elder care facility run by the Sisters of Mercy just outside Trinco (below) hope to prevent war from intruding on their humanitarian work, asking via international sign language that weapons not be brought into the home.

So was the conflict. In April 2006, when the war paid yet another visit to Trinco, the boys at Lorio's academy were told during a search that they shouldn't be on the streets.

"At least three times," Lorio said, "It was mentioned to the people here that, 'If there's any problems, we're going to shoot.' I try to keep the students inside at night; they may be shot if there are any problems."

"God doesn't require that you succeed;
He only requires that you try. "
– Agnes Gonxha Bojaxhiu, Mother Theresa of Calcutta

Chapter 8
A Priest's Journey

On the religious holidays dearest to his calling – Christmas and Easter – Father Lloyd Anthony Lorio made every attempt to communicate with people he knew from around the world.

There weren't too many international names to include; he had, of course, family in his native United States, and since the tsunami Lorio had formed friendships with a growing number of American visitors to his modest Jesuit Academy in Trincomalee. Few people make that particular voyage, and Lorio didn't leave Sri Lanka often since first arriving in 1951 for what became his life's work.

In April 2006, Lorio included Easter greetings with the e-mails he sent to American friends, volunteers from the Grace Care Center orphanage a few kilometers north of Lorio's academy on Harbour Beach Road. He typed the words carefully, with unsteady, 79-year-old hands still more familiar with a manual typewriter than the softer keyboard of a computer. His messages were often composed as old-fashioned letters once were: The hand-written variety that tried to review all the news in a communication that might take days, even weeks to reach its recipient.

Other times, Lorio's e-mails read like frantic telegrams. Along with an obligatory nod to the holiday, Lorio wrote of an explosion that week near the bus stand in Trinco's market district. The bomb killed 16 people; the aftermath included the looting and torching of local businesses.

Not long after the tsunami, roads around Trinco included a growing number of military bunkers and security checkpoints as war dominated Sri Lankan life. At times, the community struggled to maintain basic existence when hartals kept stores closed for days or even weeks at a time. As the war escalated, people in the community kept close to home and family, didn't travel at night, and stored whatever rations could be found against the next disaster.

"Perhaps as many as 40 stores were burned," Lorio reported. "It seems as if only Tamil shops were burned."

In time, reports of the latest violence became more complete, told the Sri Lankan way through word-of-mouth spread over weeks and months. A friend of Lorio's, a fellow member of the Trincomalee branch of Rotary Club International, watched as a mob destroyed his business, his trucks, and a newly acquired car belonging to his son. When some members of the crowd turned their attentions on the shop owner, the Rotarian and his son climbed over fences to escape, scrambling for their lives in the now-riotous streets of Trinco.

Sadly, Lorio accepted the realities of man's worst instincts, and continued wishing, working and praying for a better version of Trinco and Sri Lanka, a return to the peace he first encountered and still believed was possible. He remained a practical man: During his five decades of service, Lorio always knew the nearest escape route for the boys in his care as well as he had memorized the rituals of morning mass.

Lorio's electronic letter of April 2006 was brief; he was visiting another church and made use of their computer before heading back to the Academy, taking a moment to bring his friends up to date on the news.

"It is dark now," he concluded his letter. "I must go or I will have real trouble to get to the house."

That was Lorio's reality, a factor in his work and faith. He came to a land of peace and newly-declared independence, and remained in a country torn by war, poverty and ethnic violence. He'd seen children attempt poison-induced suicide, and worked in a community where the bodies of beaten, raped young girls were found on nearby roads, where they were left after being killed.

"This is my life," Lorio said, using telegraph-worthy shorthand to summarize a message more complicated than four simple words might indicate.

***

Through the mid-20th Century, the New Orleans Province of Jesuits actively supported its Ceylon Mission, sending priests on assignment to Sri Lanka for service at facilities including St. Michael's College in Batticaloa, and St. Joseph's in Trincomalee.

In the early 1950s, there was reason to believe that religious leaders could help guide the people of southern Asia societies into the modern world, with peace both a goal and strategy. The Feb. 4, 1948 declaration of Ceylon's independence from Great Britain came on the heels (and in the shadow) of India's similar proclamation of self-government, an historic milestone inspired in no small measure by Mohandas ("Mahatma") Gandhi, who achieved his goals through non-violence.

It was a lesson others thought could be applied elsewhere. When 24-year-old Lloyd Anthony Lorio arrived in Sri Lanka, he believed the island could prosper with a peaceful future for all Sri Lankans.

"All the different groups were together," Lorio said. It was a land of contrasts, where the seemingly genial nature of most Sri Lankans – distinctions between Singhalese, Tamils or Muslims were lost on most visitors – betrayed a streak of violence. In the mid-1950s, Sri Lanka carried one of the world's highest murder rates per capita; violence turned inward was equally frequent, with suicide rates near the high end of the spectrum.

Lorio was born in 1927, one of 12 children in a crowded, southern Louisiana household. When World War II ended, the young priest was serving with the New Orleans Province of Jesuits, who asked him to join the Ceylon Mission, a cause dating back to early 1500s origins under Saint Francis Xavier. At the time, the European priests were struggling to fulfill their mission.

"The ones who had been there, the French fathers, could not supply the men as was needed," Lorio said. "This was after the war, and they were short of men. So they asked for a group to continue the work they have in Ceylon. I was willing to do anything I could to help people, and I volunteered."

Although sad to leave behind a large, loving family and familiar environment, Lorio headed east with little expectation of ever returning to America. (He made three visits for family functions over the years, to attend weddings or funerals.) It was the life he was chosen for, he believed, and accepted the assignment.

In other ways, he was discouraged with the direction he saw his native country taking, a post-war America with a growing addiction to television and air conditioners, "That kept people away from each other," he sighed. Lorio hoped to spend his days in pursuit of his calling, serving as teacher, prefect and mentor on a small, impoverished island whose technology was largely still in the 1800s.

"I did not expect to go back to visit. The world was different at that time," Lorio recalled. "You did not travel the way you travel today. I expected to spend the rest of my life right here."

After arriving in Colombo, Lorio's first destination was to the island's east via a train trip considered a modern luxury: The Fathers who preceded him did not have a rail line available, and had to circle the island by sea to reach the east coast. Lorio was brought into the Society of Jesuits, first studying and working in India for five years before being ordained in 1956.

At St. Michael's in Batticaloa, Lorio was assigned to take charge of up to 90 boarding students at the boys' school, teaching during the day and serving as prefect for the dormitory. The students, he recalled, represented every facet of the population, with Singhalese and Tamils, Buddhists and Hindus seated side-by-side.

During his first year, Lorio also spent time in Trincomalee – "Just an old village at the time" – to supervise a group of young men who hoped to join the Jesuits. The dramatic changes shaping the western world for the second half of the 20th Century went unnoticed in southern Asia; in Sri Lanka, the initial expectations of independence were that young men could, for the first time, pursue crafts, trades and careers without social or caste-based limitations or restrictions.

In just a few years, Lorio said that some began doubting that the island's opportunities would be equal. He didn't witness ethnic tensions in the relative melting pots of Trincomalee and Batticaloa, but the actions of a few in Colombo signaled the origins of a conflict.

‹ death and damage near market

War and peace: In early 2006, an explosion rocked the bus station near Trinco's market district (above), 16 people including this taxi driver (supplied photo). In the aftermath of the uprising, Father Lorio's assistant, Sylvester Vasanthan (below) was taken into custody by police – with officers including friends and students of his – and was held for three months without having specific charges filed against him.

"At the time we had peace," Lorio said. "Tamil boys and Singhalese boys, there was no difficulty. The trouble started when they began to talk about 'Sinhala-only,' or about Sri Lanka being a Buddhist country; I believe most of that was for political reasons. According to Buddhism we should have real peace, but that's not the way it worked out."

First it was political, beginning with the nation's first Prime Minister, Don Stephen Senanayake, who was among the leaders of the independence movement. Senanayake died in office in 1952, and was replaced by his son, Dudley Senanayake. The Senanayake's were supported by the ruling United National Party, which established the Citizenship Act of 1948 that many felt disenfranchised Indian workers of Tamil descent.

That party lost power in 1956, and Senanayake was replaced by S.W.R.D. Bandaranaike, a UNP dissenter who established the Sri Lankan Freedom Party to promote Singhalese culture while extending state control of the economy through socialist policies. Bandaranaike was assassinated in 1959, shortly after passing the Sinhala Only Act making Sinhalese Sri Lanka's "official" language. He was replaced by his widow, Sirimavo Bandaranaike, the world's first female prime minister.

Nationalism was the philosophy as the Bandaranaike administration sought a Singhalese, Buddhist nation: All schools were under state control, and the promotion of Singhalese interests and national language left many Tamils believing that most of the (expanding number of) government-controlled positions were reserved for Singhalese residents, in an economy that favored the south and west over the northeast.

In the 1960s, political debates grew increasingly tense between parties seeking favor for Singhalese or Tamil, for considerations given to Buddhist or Hindu causes. In the early 1970s, when a revised Constitution was approved for what was now called Sri Lanka, some said the result was an institutional discrimination no better than the class or caste systems of the past. The Tamil Hindu minority pressed for more autonomy in the north and east, and political parties became

Checkpoints became familiar sights throughout Trinco, whether in the market district or at this post, outside of the Methodist Girls College where the Grace children attend school.

increasingly active, including one established in 1976, the Liberation Tigers of Tamil Eelam (LTTE).

Lorio said that, from that point, the country's direction was becoming increasingly hostile. Members of the clergy were hardly immune to the conflict. Father Eugene John Hebert, sent from Louisiana to Ceylon in 1948, was a teacher and coach in Trinco before he disappeared, along with his driver, in 1990 while en route to Batticaloa. Hebert was a member of the Batticaloa Peace Committee when he was, presumably, killed.

"You had more and more violence beginning around that time," Lorio said. "The more the civil war grew, so did the separation of people." Northern schools insisted on teaching the Tamil language to Tamil-only classrooms, Singhalese communities responded in kind. In the early 1980s, Lorio was teaching at a trade school in the southern port town, Galle, when political arguments began seeking military solutions.

The Tiger attacks on government troops in 1983 initiated weeks of Singhalese retaliations on Tamil homes and businesses in the south. "Black July," as it was known in Sri Lankan history, often called by international news agencies "the anti-Tamil riots," killed thousands of Tamil civilians in Colombo, Galle and other southern, Singhalese-majority cities. (In 2001, the Sri Lankan government told the BBC of its plans to appoint a presidential commission of inquiry to investigate who initiated the riots. No formal charges resulted from that panel.)

"I remember watching people who ran around burning stuff," said Lorio, a sad and weary witness to what became an immediate threat to the young people, boys or girls, who sought shelter inside his classrooms. "Many times, people would come over the wall of the college to go into the rooms. When the trouble came, we closed the doors and made provisions to get out on the other side. I made sure I was able to get people out, to escape if anything happened."

From a relatively safe balcony, Lorio watched as a population tried to destroy itself.

"I have seen people being burned to death," Lorio said, recalling one method of trapping a man in a tower of burning tires, of seeing people taken off a civilian bus and shot, of the sounds of explosions becoming commonplace.

"It wasn't very nice, but I've been through all that. Day by day, we do what we can to help those who are suffering."

***

In the year that followed the tsunami, the relationship between Father Lorio's academy and the children and friends of Grace Care Center grew with each new team that visited the orphanage. Visitors who spent time with Lorio quickly became as fond of his gentle, easy nature as they were impressed by the priest's dedication, which remained undaunted after 50 years of seemingly insurmountable challenges.

The relationship was also of mutual interest and common goals. Lorio's Academy struggled with a skeleton crew and a host of ideas that often remained wishful thoughts, due to the lack of funding or manpower (or, as was common in the northeast, a stable environment). Throughout 2005 Grace Care Center welcomed a steady flow of visitors who, by then, were encouraged to meet Lorio and learn more about his mission and how the needs of Grace and the Academy might coincide. Lorio's English courses, among other ideas, were suitable classes for some of the older Grace girls who were poised and able to begin learning the language. Vocational training at the academy, previously dedicated to skilled trades, gave way to the 21st Century and focused on computer skills, both hardware operations and software applications. In early 2006, Lorio's classrooms were filled with anywhere from 100 to 150 students (relocation, displacement, poverty and conflict make for an often-changing class roster) spending four hours a day for four months learning the basics of those subjects.

As the relative peace of the tsunami-recovery period faded and tensions rose, an increasing number of boys sought shelter in the small dormitories at the academy, boys whose families and homes were equally shattered by circumstance: In conjunction with another priest, a House of Peace for 17 boys soon became operational on the Academy compound. Along with a growing number of facilities in town, Lorio's academy and Grace Home were part of a struggling community with the common goal of sheltering and educating the vulnerable young.

"The boys are the ones targeted the most," said Lorio. After the bloody month that started 2006, there was a dramatic increase in the presence of security forces in Trinco, and Lorio made certain that his young charges had proper identification cards when they left the school grounds. Usually, it was better if they simply not leave the relative safety of the campus as the situation escalated with each passing month.

By April, the shelter of the school grounds was no longer a guarantee of safety. More than 30 people were reported killed in Trincomalee in the week beginning Friday, April 7, when Vanniasingham Vigneswaran, president of the Trincomalee District Tamil People's Forum – an activist group reportedly supportive of the LTTE – was shot and killed by gunmen near a downtown bank. Vigneswaran was, at the time, leading a campaign to have the controversial Buddha statue – placed there in mid-2005 and heavily guarded since – removed from Trinco's market area. He was also expected to replace parliamentarian Joseph Pararajasingham, who had been killed the previous December.

In the week that followed, there were military casualties from a string of reported Tiger attacks – at least 10 sailors and their driver were killed when their bus hit a landmine near Trinco – as well as the deaths of local police, two of whom were killed in a claymore mine ambush. Not far from Grace Care Center, Lorio reported hearing of a mine blast that killed two girls.

"People live in fear," said Lorio. "The young men ask out loud: What does the future hold for them."

The answer to that question was not optimistic after April 12, when the war came back to Trinco in explosive fashion. Army spokesmen told reporters that a claymore mine was detonated on a crowded corner near the bus stop, instantly killing a soldier and four civilians; the aftermath of rioting claimed another nine lives.

The details remained uncertain. The New York Times reported that, "An explosion at the mouth of the market killed 16 people, prompting a

Singhalese mob to instantly torch Tamil-owned shops and hunt down Tamil civilians." Singhalese villagers were reportedly slaughtered by Tamil mobs, the Times said, and, "Schools and churches have turned into squalid camps of frightened, wounded villagers."

The victims of the market blast and its aftermath, consistent with Trinco's melting pot population, included eight Tamils, five Singhalese, two Muslims and one victim who could not be identified.

Stories were told in the bloody weeks that followed: Both Singhalese and Tamil groups offered arms to villagers; a 45-year-old woman in a rice field watched six uniformed gunmen slowly march through the paddy. They motioned her to stay back before shooting six men, including the woman's younger brother. The BBC reported the same story in reverse, as claims were made that the Tamil Tigers were marching through rice fields and executing civilians. In another retaliation attack, four Tamils and a Singhalese man were killed – shot, stabbed or burned to death. Men were seen beating a small boy on a bicycle with logs before dragging him into the bushes.

At Grace Care Center, manager Diane McLaughlin was told that more than a dozen young girls "Were taken from Koneswaram Temple and chopped into pieces," and that a relative of a Mercy Home staff member was beheaded during a riot at the market.

Lorio heard the stories from many sources, from fellow clerics with whom he'd shared Easter Sunday, from McLaughlin and Hiram Labrooy at the Grace Care Center, and from the students and assistants at his academy, including Sylvester Vasanthan, an eager young man planning to, hopefully someday, continue his medical studies while working and teaching at the academy. Two days after the market blast, Vasanthan told Lorio that houses were burning in a village not far from the academy, and they'd both heard talk of the girls found on the road who had been raped before being killed.

What newspapers called a "Slide toward war" was played out with Trincomalee caught, literally, in the middle. A suicide bombing in Colombo that killed eight people during an attack on Sri Lanka's military chief prompted retaliatory air strikes on Tiger targets in

Sampoor and Muttur, each less than 15 miles from the Grace Care Center. In Trinco, security forces stepped up their presence, soldiers traded the casual-duty soft caps for steel-pot helmets; flak vests were worn continuously despite the heat.

It wasn't the Trinco that Lorio believed in: He wasn't alone in the feeling that the groups responsible for the market bombing (and most of the mob-induced looting and burning in the aftermath) were committed by people who did not live in Trinco.

"There's a fair amount of evidence that the group was brought in from outside of Trincomalee," Lorio said. (Witnesses reported seeing the original group arriving in a truck.) "Each side blames the other. People are giving up. They don't see how peace is going to happen. There are so many incidents like this."

***

By the end of April 2006, Father Lorio's concern for the community, and the nation, was focused on a single individual.

At about 3 p.m. on Sunday, April 23, several vehicles parked on Harbour Road in front of Lorio's academy, out of which came men wearing a variety of uniforms, both military and police. The local forces were not unfamiliar with the academy: Included in the group was the assistant superintendent of police, who had been taking computer courses, taught by Sylvester Vasanthan, Lorio's 25-year-old assistant and teacher.

Vasanthan's English skills had previously been put to use when he worked for the navy; he was well known in Trinco, having lived there with his family since 1990. At various times – notably after the family home was burned during the 1990s when Indian troops temporarily added an additional source of gunfire to the war – Vasanthan and his family considered leaving Sri Lanka. On his own, he had the opportunity to go to England, but, in early 2006, he explained that Sri Lanka was his home.

"I would like to help our area and people," Vasanthan said. "Everybody wants to go to Colombo to study, but we must try to make this place work, to learn English. There are people here who are poor, and cannot spend much money. We have to make peace through education."

Vasanthan was on hand when the police told Lorio they believed a claymore mine had been placed on the neighboring compound, and that they needed to search the premises. Lorio opened the gate to allow them in, and asked Vasanthan to use his mobile phone and tell two other priests from a nearby school to come to the academy. One, Father V. Yogeswaran, was able to reach the compound, located across an athletic field from his office; the other was unable to get there as the roads were blocked.

At about 4:30, they all heard a bomb explode, and Lorio assumed that the troops had detonated the device they were looking for. Instead, Lorio was told, the explosion injured a soldier.

Lorio was told that Vasanthan would be questioned about the phone call he made. Vasanthan was taken into custody by the police, which included the officer who had been his student in a computer classroom. (Vasanthan's knowledge of computers and the Internet, Lorio said, simply made him a stronger suspect.) He watched as his trusted young assistant was put in a vehicle and driven to the police station.

The days became a blur for the nearly 80-year-old priest. On Monday, Lorio was told Vasanthan would remain in custody for three days while he was investigated for possible criminal activities. On Tuesday, police said they had a Detention Order under the nation's Emergency Regulations, and that Vasanthan would be held for up to three months, likely in Colombo.

Lorio was beside himself with concern, especially after it was said that the soft-spoken young man would be transferred to the "Fourth Floor of the Investigation Center," a location of near mythical reputation as a place where suspected terrorists were taken, a place from which people do not return.

In the painful weeks to follow, the lack of news regarding Vasanthan's situation was filled with continued warfare in and around Trinco. From Grace Care Center, McLaughlin described air strikes on May 11 that included dozens of "launches," sending artillery into Muttur. While the return-to-war drew closer, Lorio and friends of Grace Care Center reached out to whatever contacts could be found to get Vasanthan released.

Lorio sent an official appeal: "I have personally known Vasanthan for three years. He has been staying in this institution and assisting in its administration. I can certify that he is honest, loyal and a law-abiding person. I am certain he has never been involved in any unlawful activities."

(Detention in Sri Lanka cast more than just doubt about the individual in custody. While in Colombo, Diane McLaughlin attempted to visit Vasanthan, but was told she would have to hand over her contact information, her passport and other papers; once registered as a visitor to a suspect, she was told she might be pulled in for questioning at any time. Lorio and McLaughlin's friends advised her to wait, given that Vasanthan was scheduled to be released without further complications.)

The three-month detention order held. Lorio was able to see Vasanthan on one occasion in Colombo, a brief visit that offered the beginning of hope. Although no formal charges were brought against Vasanthan, the weeks passed and, after the three months allowed by law, he was released.

He was told that, if he was arrested again, they would shoot him.

***

"Sri Lanka could be one of the best countries in the world," said Father Lloyd Anthony Lorio in February 2008. "It's a beautiful country, the weather is good, and the land is very kind."

The people, however, don't always match the generosity of the land, a sad acceptance for a priest approaching his 80th birthday, who wondered if he would again see the peace he first encountered in Sri Lanka.

In July 2006, McLaughlin attended a church service in Trinco with Vasanthan, a young man now struggling to grow facial hair to change his appearance, who was being told by everyone who loved him, knew him, cared for his well being, to leave the country.

"I hugged him until he was purple," McLaughlin said, an embrace both of greeting and departure, as Vasanthan reluctantly followed the advice he'd been given. When an opportunity came his way in August, he left Sri Lanka to begin a new life in Europe.

"Many of us were worried," Lorio said. "His uncle was shot a couple of weeks ago. Pray," Lorio told his friends in America. "We need peace."

Lorio continued sending holiday greetings whenever possible; a Christmas morning telephone call to America was made possible by a cellular telephone, used by a man whose earliest days in Trinco were in a town that hadn't yet received telecommunications. He spoke to Vasanthan that day as well, sad to hear a friend sound so distant, relieved to still hear his voice.

It could have been an easier life for Father Lorio, somewhere other than a struggling coastal town that, in spite of cell phones and Internet connections, still sends its fishermen to battle the waves in small rowboats using hand-casted nets, where the market welcomes farmers bringing produce to town via ox cart.

For more than 50 years, Lorio has watched generations of young Sri Lankans work together as boys only to find reasons to fight as men. The boys, he said, are the most vulnerable, but he knows they're not the only ones in a war that doesn't distinguish between civilian and combatant, adult or child, boy or girl. As a man with unshakable faith that peace is possible, the potential of Sri Lanka is the same held by the world.

"The world is suffering so much because of violence," Lorio said, "not only in Sri Lanka; but all over. If the money that is wasted on war were spent on something positive, how much happier would everyone in the world be. The world is giving so much, but we're not utilizing it as we should. We have to work together."

Under the best of circumstances, the challenge to men of the cloth is to instill faith in a divine plan, belief that today's suffering is part of the path toward future reward.

Applying that to the young people of Sri Lanka, Lorio said, is all but a lost cause:

"They don't know what to expect tomorrow."

It Takes a Village to Jump Start an Engine

"This is a pretty big bus," I said, always ready to state the obvious.

The Grace Care Center school bus – a prized asset only recently acquired to replace a smaller vehicle fondly known as the "bondo bus" for its rusting, barely-held together shell – wasn't ready for that morning's trip to Methodist Girls College. The driver repeatedly pushed the ignition key in a futile attempt to start the fading motor.

It wasn't unexpected: The engine was long in need of an overhaul, but we thought (hoped) it might be capable of a few more trips before it was time for the shop. The repair work would be an inconvenience, and an expense, but that was for later; that morning, getting the girls to school depended upon if the engine would respond to a jump start, a temporary fix that, in turn, relied upon our being able to push several tons worth of machine with sufficient speed to pop the clutch.

That's when I observed, and commented on, the size of the vehicle, and the fact that I was one of just three men on hand (other than the driver, who would necessarily be inside the bus): Hiram Labrooy was present and accounted for, as was Colin Loomis, a college student from Michigan who joined our team for a trip to Grace in February 2006. Cultural chauvinism aside, there weren't enough adult women on hand, either, for us to consider pushing the bus with the people we had available.

Diane McLaughlin, by then familiar with making daily adjustments to her schedule as manager of Grace Care Center, put aside her morning's checklist to focus on getting the girls to school. While we talked about the options, Labrooy and our driver were having other conversations.

A few men, at first, walked into the orphanage compound, soon joined by others as word spread through the informal, somewhat mysterious grapevine

Men at work: Trincomalee's fishing industry – struggling since the tsunami – suffered further under restrictions in the wake of attacks conducted by the Sea Tigers, the maritime branch of the LTTE. Informal partnerships were formed to pool resources during limited opportunities to bring food to Trinco's markets.

that kept the surrounding villages in tune with each other. Some were from the neighboring community, a four-acre camp for displaced families adjacent to Grace Care Center; some were parents dropping off toddlers for day care; others just seemed to show up as needed. However they came, the goal was the same, and in relatively short order we had a dozen or so men with a common purpose.

It wasn't easy, but with some time and effort, some internationally-understood grunts and groans (and – presumably – a mild curse or two of frustration) we had the bus rolling up the entrance road. Once started, we built up a reasonable pace, and the driver slammed the clutch and hit the gas. It took several attempts, each time the engine coughed and sputtered, rocked and rattled in short bursts, before catching hold. We collectively stumbled when the accelerator finally did its job, and the bus sped away from our shoving arms.

A cheer went up, from those pushing the vehicle and the Grace staff that stood to the side when the bus's width would accept no more help. The men shook our hands; we showed them how to "high five." The children smiled (although, one would assume, at least a few of the students were disappointed that the unexpected day without school was not in the plans). The girls climbed aboard, the men walked back up the entrance road, returning to their interrupted chores now that the crisis – harmless and innocent as it was – had passed.

Just another morning in Trinco, in many ways. The daily routine resumed its schedule at Grace Care Center. Pre-school age children in tiny, candy-stripe jumpsuits shuffled past the departing villagers who had helped send the bus on its way; the small kitchen staff – having first served breakfast before packing nearly 100 lunches for the girls – began cleaning up before they would start preparing the evening meal; Mercy Home's aging residents went about the few modest chores they could handle. McLaughlin, who had set aside a checklist of administrative tasks to ensure that the children made it to school, wished that every emergency could be dispatched as easily.

Most weren't, but the sense of community in Trinco gave birth to a neighborhood atmosphere near the district known as Uppuvelli, a postal

Dozens of children pack into the seats of the Grace Care bus (above) for the daily trip to school. Along nearby village trails (below) near Grace, a strong sense of community has helped families, neighbors and friends survive war, poverty and disaster, often within the same week.

address simply identified as "3rd Milepost." We'd come to know some of the people living in Alles Gardens, the camp for displaced families that was established even before the tsunami added to its population. In Sri Lanka's northeast, two decades of war destroyed countless communities: For every one of the hundreds of semi-organized camps established by foreign (and some internal) organizations, an equal number were developed in crude fashion by the civilians themselves, with communal bathing facilities little more than a bare pipe splashing a shower. The previous homes of hundreds of thousands of civilians were no longer safe, if they existed at all.

An informal community – absent of official declaration yet swelling with a sense of neighborhood – developed out of necessity among schools and orphanages, camps and hospitals, relief agencies and others. A kindness offered one year to the people of Alles Gardens by a visiting American was recalled each time their paths crossed, with offers of food or drink, of friendship and gratitude. It was a pleasure, they implied, to help us muscle a tired old bus engine back to life.

It was the same story throughout Trincomalee, a way of life as much as a means of survival. When the tsunami hit, it was argued that those living in makeshift camps made an easier adjustment to losing what little they had than those who had been more comfortable in their surroundings. The tsunami, at least, went away after ravaging the shoreline, and the people could start over again.

Some things kept coming back. The same sense of community needed for such mundane challenges as pushing a vehicle and getting children to school would be crucial when the war came back to Trinco. Access to basic necessities required a community to take care of itself; but first they had to survive the battle.

Chapter 9
The Wonder Twins in Trinco

There was no point in telling lies to the children of Grace Home, girls who, at times, were easy audiences for the charms of myths and legends.

Although seemingly innocent, they were also well-schooled in life's harshest lessons, and knew that the nearby explosions they heard meant that people were getting killed. Neither Diane McLaughlin nor the American visitors tried to tell the children that the sounds were anything other than war. The noises were familiar, yet signaled a more immediate concern than they'd had in recent memory.

"This time it was different," McLaughlin said, a voice experienced by eight months of watching Sri Lankan history being written, eight months of "crisis management" being a daily – hourly – chore.

This was more than just a singular emergency or remote tragedy. For the better part of a week in early August 2006, explosions and bombs could be heard around-the-clock, screaming overhead en route to a Tiger compound just north of the orphanage and, in turn, from artillery pounding the village of Muttur just south of the harbor.

To the children, McLaughlin could answer – honestly if not completely – that although the explosions sounded pretty close, the targets were people and places other than Grace Home. It was a half-hearted fairy tale; half believed by children whose innocence was long ago a wartime casualty.

To her American friends, however, McLaughlin was more direct:

"We are seriously under attack."

It didn't take long for Mercy Home to fulfill its potential, with bonds formed between the elders and the girls of Grace Home. That sense of familial love and loyalty were frequently – desperately – needed when the war came back to Trinco.

***

The people of Trincomalee were, in many ways, surprised when the war came to town. For more than two decades, much of the conflict had been fought either in the far north or closer to Colombo. Although much of the eastern district was said to have been "controlled" by the LTTE, Trinco remained a relatively stable environment, watched over by a variety of government security forces. Conflict-related incidents that happened nearby were thought to be on the fringe of the war.

That changed in January 2006. The shooting deaths of five students – a crime destined to remain unresolved in court – were generally perceived to have been sanctioned by the government, amounting to an act of war. In the months that followed, dozens of incidents were created by both sides (and by a growing number of splinter, paramilitary groups), with mounting fatalities.

Hopes were fading that the war would soon end; the latest discouragement was the canceled peace talks scheduled in April. In May, President Mahinda Rajapakse appointed new members of the Human Rights Commission, although Amnesty International said the commission, "Appeared no longer to comply fully with constitutional and international standards for human rights institutions." Countries belonging to the European Common Union listed the LTTE as a terrorist organization, prohibited entry to Tiger officers, and froze some of the group's international assets.

The world might not have agreed on who was committing the most war crimes, but there was little doubt as to the true victims. UNICEF reported that, "Sri Lankan children … are paying a high price for the escalating tension on the island." In late May, the BBC interviewed Rev. Dr. S. Jeyanesan, the inspiration and overseas agent for VeAhavta and Grace Care Center, who joined an international appeal for the leadership of Sri Lanka to halt the war. Jeyanesan described the number of orphanages run by the Church of South India, and the increasing violence that created additional homeless children.

"The children were hiding, as they thought another war is on the way," said Rev. Jey. "Not only are they very scared, they have lost hope on the future. Safeguarding the children, educating and feeding them, should be the priorities of a society. I blame both sides. I appeal to both parties to stop these killings in the name of the children."

Neither children – nor adults – would be completely safe in the months that followed. On June 15, along a narrow, desolate stretch of road in the north central Anuradapura province, a claymore mine was detonated, ripping through a civilian passenger bus. More than 60 riders were killed, including 15 children; more than 70 others were injured.

The government issued a now-routine statement that the Tigers detonated the mine; that press release was followed by a denial from the LTTE. Within hours of the attack on the bus, Sri Lankan Air Force jets were en route to the Tiger's Jaffna base, where bombs were dropped in and near Killinochchi.

About 100 kilometers separates Anuradapura and Trinco, but silent echoes from the bus explosion were felt, if not heard. Tension blanketed the streets, already smothered by the mid-summer heat and humidity. From the vantage point of Grace Care Center, McLaughlin heard of villagers who were asked by officials to leave their homes. After recent shellings in the jungles bordering Trinco, McLaughlin said that 50 wandering Lankans sought shelter at Grace, scaling the walls to find safety inside in spite of the brick barrier topped with embedded shards of broken glass. The potentially painful climb, they knew, was less risky than the open gunfire and grenade explosions at the end of the entrance road, less than 100 meters away. Gunshots, McLaughlin said, had become practically a daily occurrence. What few doubts that some of Trinco's population may have held all but disappeared.

"Not one person I have spoken to believes there will be peace," McLaughlin said.

McLaughlin's friends, in Ohio or Colombo, made countless suggestions that she leave the war-torn region, passionate advice, guided

A country of contrasts: Diane McLaughlin enjoys a moment (above) with a baby from a nearby village, whose family was taking a (rare) peaceful walk along the beach adjacent to Grace. Away from the orphanage (below), the cease-fire agreement between the government and the LTTE faded fast in 2006, as Sri Lanka edged closer to all-out war.

by love and concern. "They think I've lost my marbles," McLaughlin said. "That I'm taking unnecessary risks. I can't explain to them that I'm safe."

On days when McLaughlin could "feel the shake" from a claymore mine blast near the access road, she remained convinced that Grace – through some quirk of fate or luck of location – was somehow not at risk.

"All I can do is help those surrounding me," she said, "and not worry about what's going on outside."

The stories from "outside," however, were as painful to hear as the bombastic, nerve-shattering shock waves of nearby explosions were to feel. Stories were told: Of the decapitation-by-machete of a young boy; a three-wheel taxi driver shot to death after being pulled over at a check point; two girls who were tied up for death by hanging – a crime committed in the same hut where their mother was raped and shot. Reportedly, the children had also been sexually abused. (Photographs of the teenage girls appeared in a Tamil language newspaper, heads bent unnaturally to the side, their dead mother in the shadows behind them.)

"Things are getting more and more gruesome every day," McLaughlin said.

A new security checkpoint – recently installed near Trinco's downtown – was blown up in early July. Seven security troops were killed, and 15 others, including civilians, were injured. A makeshift explosive was timed for detonation and hidden in a tuk-tuk that was parked near the military post.

"It was very, very loud," said McLaughlin, who was within earshot of the incident. "They're getting very creative with their devices."

Military officers visited Grace, and described the orphanage as a "safe zone" that would be protected whenever possible. Roads to and from the compound, however, were not always under such declared security.

Typically, it wasn't just herself, or even the children and elders under her charge that concerned McLaughlin. She wondered about

"Wonder Twin" Erin Whaley (above) shares a moment with friends Satheka (left) and Tharshala during a February 2006 visit. During Whaley's subsequent trip that summer, the orphanage was caught in the crossfire during a clash between a Tiger camp to the north and the village of Muttur to the south. After the bombings and counter-attacks, the bodies of 17 relief workers (below) were found, their deaths determined to have been caused by close-range gunfire. (Supplied photo.)

the group from America that was expected in just a few weeks: Would they make it through, and, assuming they reached Trinco, would they be able to leave. A growing number of international relief workers and monitors were leaving the district, if not the country. Other teams had cancelled, and she knew that the late July team from California and Michigan might be forced to postpone their trip.

She should have known better. Included in this team was, after all, her "twin."

***

When Erin Whaley, a 28-year-old middle school teacher from southeast Michigan, made her first trip to Grace Care Center, it was to a place she felt she'd known as well as the small town she called home.

By then, she'd spent nearly eight months learning about the orphanage, memorizing photographs taken by Ann Arbor-area visitors, and studying the troubles surrounding Trinco. In January 2005, her community launched a series of tsunami-inspired fund-raisers, ranging from modest donations of returnable cans and bottles collected by children (including Whaley's students), to a music concert that concluded the effort. Instead of contributing relief money to a broader, international organization, the "South Lyon to Sri Lanka" effort raised funds that would go directly to VeAhavta and Grace Care Center. A connection was formed, and those involved witnessed – first hand – how that assistance was put to work.

During that summer's break from her school obligations, Whaley joined a seven-member group – two of whom previously visited Grace in February – that included Diane McLaughlin. The two met in August 2005 at Detroit's Metro Airport, and during the 48-hour door-to-door trip, Whaley and McLaughlin found many common interests, shared with the comfortable conversation flow that sparks rapid friendships. While at Grace, without planning to, the pair dressed in matching colors or combinations, wardrobe choices that, coupled with a deepening bond, invited the nickname, "The Wonder Twins," borrowed from a television superhero program from their similar-aged childhoods.

After that first visit (during which the group wondered about the possibility of war when Foreign Minister Lakshman Kadirgamar was assassinated), Whaley returned to a suburban classroom while McLaughlin made life-altering plans. By the time McLaughlin returned to Grace to become the orphanage's full-time manager, the Wonder Twins had become daily e-mail, text or phone companions. The one-year anniversary of their initial meeting approached, with anxious phone calls counting the hours until their reunion in Trinco. McLaughlin shared her cross-planetary phone calls with some of the children. In America, Whaley heard small, familiar voices describe the sounds of war.

"They just had a bomb explode, and they were asking me how I was doing," Whaley said "They asked: 'When you come to Sri Lanka?'" She told her friends she would be there soon.

The team – Whaley, Mercy Home co-planner Cheryl Huckins, VeAhavta board member, Pastor Greg Hill, and Tom McLaughlin, a physical therapist from California – arrived on July 26. During their first few days in country, the visitors enjoyed playing with the girls, catching up with old friends, and meeting new ones.

Early into their stay, Whaley, McLaughlin and Huckins visited the girls' school one morning. Walking the grounds with the principal, they spotted more than a few hands waving out of classroom windows, "Laughing, like kids anywhere when visitors come to their school," Huckins said.

The visitors returned to Grace. A few hours later, an explosion was heard just outside of the Methodist Girls College. Soldiers swarmed the school gate and grounds, armed and ready. Trinco was closed for business, an emergency hartal shut down the roads.

At Grace, McLaughlin and Whaley made the decision to take the bus to the school and bring the children back to the orphanage.

McLaughlin feared that the "plan" of having the students remain at the school overnight would, in reality, extend beyond a day or two. She preferred to get them out of Trinco proper before further escalation could put them in more immediate danger. (Memories of the January shooting deaths of five students still guided a decision or two in Trinco. It proved to be the right call: The next day, a school not far from Grace Home was hit by a grenade attack that killed 10 civilians among the hundreds who sought shelter inside.)

McLaughlin, Whaley and a driver from Grace Home ignored the speed limit. Checkpoints were driven through, the guards allowing uninterrupted passage to McLaughlin's, "White hand waving out the window. It was kinda funny," she said, "bouncing past checkpoints so fast. I thought we were going to be up on two wheels."

The checkpoints were just one potential danger. More than 20 jets roared overhead, ordinance rained from the sky and was answered with counter-attacks, retaliations and civil unrest on the streets, which included countless blasts of small-arms fire, grenades and homemade explosives.

"I've been through the drill before, but this was different," McLaughlin said. Helicopters joined larger aircraft in the tropical sky while too-many-to-count blasts were heard nearby. "This time, it was us getting hit." Trinco was, as McLaughlin said, "Seriously under attack."

McLaughlin, Whaley and dozens of frightened but happy children made it back to Grace. That evening, when the sun disappeared behind the jungles to the west, a classroom's worth of the youngest children gathered in McLaughlin's room. Her modest quarters in the guest houses, designed to provide basic accommodations for visitors, included precious few creature comforts: no television or air conditioning against the long hours or blazing heat. Yet there was a sense of security; the walls were decorated with pictures of family and friends and a well-rendered painting of a pole fisherman, recently bought on a rare day of luxury. The cozy room was an ideal place to tell a nighttime story to sleepy children.

Eric Parkinson, wrestling with the same fears but burdened by distance, was in near-constant communication with Grace. McLaughlin passed a cell phone around the room for a few brief words to be exchanged; Parkinson's gentle, comforting voice offered love and support both on the phone and, often that week, via bedtime stories he and his wife, Sharon, had recorded which McLaughlin played for the girls. Children, elders, staff and visitors waited out the night, drifting at times into short stretches of sleep, before a particularly loud blast ended the pretense.

Even the sense of safety at the orphanage was rare that week. The peaceful complex became a seven-acre bunker, sheltering children, elders, friends and neighbors who sought safety within its walls.

"Sri Lanka rebels say war back on," read the Reuter's headline. Seven soldiers and three Tigers were killed Monday, July 31, during what was described as the first Sri Lankan military advance into "rebel-held territory" since the 2002 cease fire. Although the government controlled much of the Eastern District, parts of Batticaloa were held by the LTTE. Tiger political leader S. Elilan said that government troops and Tigers were battling over control of land from Trinco down to Batticaloa.

Specifically, the fighting was over control of a water sluice operation located just outside Muttur, a seaside village south of the harbor from Trinco. On Aug. 2, the water gate was taken over by the LTTE. The government, conversely, said that the rebels tried to capture the jetty, but that the Sri Lankan Navy defeated these attempts. (Either way, before a significant push by government forces to recapture and re-open the gate, an estimated 50,000 residents had no access to water.)

Daily combat followed. The Tigers took their suicide attack methods to sea by ramming a fishing boat loaded with explosives into a troop transport ship. Tiger artillery was fired at Trincomalee harbor; Air Force jets bombed rebel positions just to the north and south of the orphanage, an onslaught that lasted for seven straight days.

Reports came in daily, too disturbing to think about, too many to confirm. McLaughlin and Whaley watched the nighttime sky light up with flares and missiles when the three Navy camps closest to the orphanage – the nearest being less than a mile north along the beach – were hit with Tiger artillery.

"The sound was enormous," McLaughlin said, who ended another day with no certainty of tomorrow, on a third world beach with a friend she'd met just one year earlier. Both women first traveled to Sri Lanka on an impulse to help, they thought, a disaster-recovery project in an impoverished region. A year later, the Wonder Twins felt as if they had enlisted in a war together.

"As it stands now," Norwegian peace envoy Jon Hanssen-Bauer told Reuter's reporter Peter Apps in early August. "There is no reason for any kind of optimism."

For every missile launched by conventional aircraft or artillery in remote, anonymous combat, retaliations and "isolated incidents" took a more personal approach on the streets. A Mercy Home staffer, a young man who worked as an orderly at the residence for elders, heard the faint yet sharp whistle of close-call bullets when he was targeted for potshots while riding a scooter to work. (He, and others, would join the "overnight" guest list at Grace that week.)

***

When the sounds finally slowed to a non-threatening level, an exhausted community of children, elders and staff retreated to their rooms for a restless sleep on a hot afternoon. For the past week, they had clung to the restricted safety of the compound, other than temporary escapes from the war with a "sea bath" in the Bay of Bengal.

"They can't hear the bombs while they're in the ocean," McLaughlin said. The once-threatening waves that brought the tsunami now offered a distraction from disasters more man-made than natural.

A group of visitors and staff left the orphanage for the first time in days, their destination to have dinner at a small guest house that neighbored Grace. Cheryl Huckins noticed the difference between being inside the Grace property and the world just outside its gates. The metal barrier swung open, a rusted hinge protesting through an arc wide enough for motor vehicle passage. The sounds shifted as they walked away from the ocean and crows and within range of howling dogs and street noise; faint, yet nearby gunshots echoed off the cinderblock walls of the small homes lining the entrance road.

"This is the background they live in," Huckins said, who watched a community's collective resiliency during the onslaught. The elders of Mercy Home – having long since transformed the planned nursing facility into a vital, active environment, went about their chores, kept the children calm, and turned a deaf ear to sounds they'd heard for decades.

The results of the latest chapter in the war were being tallied. Lives became numbers, whether in the reports of 10,000 suffering refugees in one village, or another 10,000 in worse condition across the bay in Kinniya, "Numbers as big as the tsunami," Huckins said. Fatalities were mounted in groups – 10 civilians were killed one day by artillery fire – or in scattered, individual incidents, adding up to more than 150 victims in the immediate area within a few short days. July and August would clearly be the bloodiest months in Sri Lanka since the 2002 cease fire.

The incident which caused the most concern during that period was the shooting deaths on Aug. 4 of 17 relief workers in Muttur, killed by close-range gunshot – not, as originally reported, "Collateral" damage from the aerial attacks that blanketed the region. Their bloating corpses lay in the heat for two days before being discovered. Reuter's called it, "The highest toll for a single incident since the 2003 bombing of the United Nation's offices in Baghdad."

The victims – 16 Tamil and one Muslim – worked for the French agency, "Action Contre La Faim" (Action Against Hunger), which had been serving in Muttur since 1997. Most of the victims wore a t-shirt signaling their affiliation with the agency.

"The government and the Tamil Tigers have traded blame for the killings," the New York Times reported. There was plenty of blame to trade; political maneuverings were made from both directions as the war escalated after the bodies were found. Military personnel were killed in dozens of attacks, and a gunboat chase on Aug. 9 turned the harbor into a maritime battleground. After that, navy boat rounded up the fishermen and escorted them back to shore, and the government imposed the first of many restrictions on fishing, a ban advertised as in the interest of safety, yet often perceived as suppression of the struggling communities in the northeast.

Not for the first – or last – time, reports of the conflict could not be taken at face value. The absence of the media's access to legitimate information gave birth to unconfirmed numbers that, when added up by reporters, exceeded possibility, let alone probability. Along with inflated numbers of battlefield kills, press releases from both sides charged the other with causing civilian deaths: More than 50 civilians were reported killed on Aug. 10; the LTTE blamed the murders on the government, in response to previous accusations that were made against the Tigers. (Overall, the reports of persons killed reflected a fraction of deaths that went unacknowledged. Buried in the same news archives as recent deaths were reports of mass graves being discovered, each of which clarified a few more of the countless "disappearances" over the years.)

For one family, the shooting deaths of relief workers in Muttur added yet another tragedy. Ponuthurai Yogarajah, 62, lost a son in Muttur, just eight months after another son, Yogarajah Hemachandran, was one of the five students killed in Trincomalee.

"There is no use living," Yogarajah told Reuter's. "It would be better to have died before them."

(In April 2008, watchdog group University Teachers for Human Rights, in conjunction with Human Rights Watch, released a statement that local security troops were responsible for the Muttur shootings. Reportedly, the brother of a home guard had been killed by a Tiger gunman, and the guard vowed revenge. When the shelling started, security forces were ordered to "finish off" Tamil-speaking citizens, regardless of civilian clothing, and bloody, misdirected revenge was enacted under cover of open warfare. James Ross, senior legal advisor to Human Rights Watch, called the official government investigation, "Little more than a bad joke played out on the victims' families and the international community.")

The latest round of war wasn't over yet. On Aug. 14, in the northern district Mullaittivu, near the Tiger base in Jaffna, more than 60 children – teenage girls, mostly – were killed by missiles fired from government jets. The function of the targeted facility was subject to debate: Headlines called it an 'orphanage,' others called it a Tiger training camp. Accusations flew across disconnected media channels, news reports, and Internet sites. Again, it was promised that investigations would be conducted.

The result was the same, regardless of the purpose of the facility: Another 60-plus children lost their lives to the conflict.

***

"If it weren't for the NGOs," Father Lloyd Anthony Lorio told Erin Whaley, "These people would be starving."

Lorio and his Jesuit Academy, among many others throughout Trinco, worked with volunteer groups from around the world to help those fleeing the war's latest theater. As the days passed, McLaughlin was able to recognize "an isolated explosion" that was not "directly related to the war," a minor yet telling detail.

With the immediate threat of war removed, assistance to those in need took on all shapes, forms and possibilities, sometimes from unlikely (yet fitting) sources. A few months earlier, the families in the makeshift "Alles Gardens" camp next to Grace had relocated, on a hill about a kilometer north of the orphanage. Houses built by a Korean Christian group welcomed the families to a small neighborhood of modest yet solid, functioning homes. When news spread around town that people who fled Muttur were in search of refuge, those same families made the trip down the hill to offer surplus supplies and food to those in need, some of whom set up temporary accommodations in the former camp. They worked with Grace's in-resident pastor, Rev. Gnanapragasm, to funnel donations wherever needed. (An ambulance driver told Huckins that up to 20,000 refugees had fled Muttur for neighborhoods in Trinco and Kinniya.)

The communities surrounding Trincomalee struggled for basic survival in the aftermath of the latest combat actions: Supply channels had been disrupted; countless homes in Muttur, in spite of a reopened water sluice, were laid to rubble as so many were during the tsunami; a hospital in Muttur had been nearly destroyed; stores were closed, making basic necessities difficult to obtain; thousands of villagers from south of the bay sought shelter in the communities of Trinco.

McLaughlin and Whaley felt humbled when they met with an informal, inter-agency group in Trinco, including representatives of both small organizations and "the big dogs," as McLaughlin called UNICEF, Oxfam and others, who spoke in expansive terms of bringing significant amounts of assistance to the area.

"I feel like chump change compared to the help these guys can bring," McLaughlin said. (A falsely modest statement given the dedication and responsibility she lived on a daily basis.) Throughout August, the Wonder Twins, Hiram Labrooy and Rev. Gnanapragasm operated an informal staging area, as donations and scavenged supplies were distributed based on need throughout Trinco.

Along the east coast, the situation was often called a "humanitarian crisis." The United Nations, International Red Cross and other agencies stopped trying to count casualties and survivors; even the most conservative guess revealed a severe hardship created by just two days of combat. An estimated 200,000 people had been displaced in eastern Sri Lanka just in the April-August period. That population joined the nearly half million souls who remained without shelter and basic services since the tsunami nearly two years earlier.

"These are all lives, not numbers," said Rev. Jeyanesan, who organized relief and medical projects operating out of St. John's in Batticaloa. "We really do not know the numbers of injured and the refugee population."

When the roads were open, Grace staff and other local groups distributed supplies to compounds filled far beyond capacity. Schools built to accommodate 300 students now served as shelter to 6,000 people. Two schools in Trinco held a thousand families each. The Mercy Mobile Clinic – among the early VeAhavta projects in pre-tsunami days – was re-activated to make visits to these new camps.

Elsewhere, the war-in-all-but-name included a week of open combat near Jaffna, in what one analyst called, "World War I-style" ground fighting: Neither side moving, neither advancing nor retreating, just shooting at one another with neither gain nor purpose as nearly a thousand troops were reportedly killed. Both sides announced to the world that they would honor the terms of the cease-fire, but the reality in Sri Lanka told a different story.

"They claim it's not war," Whaley said as her time at Grace Care Center came to an end, in an electronic message with sentences occasionally interrupted by the word "bomb" written between parentheses, reflecting the soundtrack just beyond the peaceful orphanage grounds.

On Aug. 21, members of the Nordic-based Sri Lanka Monitoring Mission left the dangerous northeast to reconsider their options in Colombo. Earlier that year, those same peace-keepers, and many NGOs, made the decision of safety against a seemingly futile mission, and temporarily left the area. (By September, the SLMM made its final departure from Sri Lanka.) Some went reluctantly, but were under too many orders from parent organizations to remain.

Diane McLaughlin remained in Trinco, watching the resources for peace fade away one agency at a time.

"If the peace-keepers are run out of town, what will happen next," McLaughlin asked.

Encounters
Cry Uncle (the Indian Ocean Blues)

One of the older Grace Home girls, Ushna, was clearly hesitant about stepping out further into the sea.

A beautiful kid – Ushna could have been the basis for a princess in a Disney musical romance – she was a shy, sweet, quiet girl of 17, and by her nature a bit uncomfortable in the water. In the spirit of Grace Girl unity, she bravely joined the "sea bath," taking small, delicate, lady-like, steps into the waves, flinching when spirited, nearby splashing threatened to get her wet before she was good and ready. (This, of course, made it all the more fun to douse her and bring her further into the water, where the laughter of children soon dominated over the ocean's roar.)

Her discomfort had nothing to do with being haunted by the waves, with memories of the destruction they'd brought just eight months earlier. Our sea bath that August afternoon was the first time the children had been in the ocean since the tsunami. The youngest among them seemed to have the easiest time getting reacquainted with the simple, precious art of playing in water; for others, the memories of the deadly waves were still too fresh. At first, they kept their distance on the beach, waiting to confirm that nothing bad was going to happen.

The oceanic pool party was, in part, a spur-of-the-moment plan. Visitors from America – themselves anxious to add "swam in Indian Ocean" to their diary of south Asian adventures – understood that the children had been away from the water long enough. The people of Trincomalee needed to come to terms with the ocean that greatly helped define their lives: Earlier that year, fishermen said more than a few prayers when forced, by necessity, to take on the sea not long after the disaster. As the months passed, the children had to put nightmare images in the past, and realize that (unlike the

Visitors recognized Grace Home girl Ushna Kristhamoothry for her quiet beauty, shy nature and studious manner. Among the first girls to call Grace "home," Ushna served as a leader and role model to the younger children.

unpredictable horrors of war) the sea would not pay another deadly visit to their home.

Nature took its course; a very wet therapy session turned into basic playtime, and we happily splashed in the waves with dozens of children. Water balloons were filled and tossed, a game to see how many throws could be made before it burst (yet hoping for the moment when a laughing face was playfully doused with water); a beach ball (a near requisite gift from the California group) bounced from one cluster to another; smaller children jumped on the backs of the laughing visitors.

Ushna was among the last to join, and I coaxed her, step-by-step, toward the point of no return. She smiled, as she had when I told her simple, pun-filled riddles; jokes designed for a much younger audience. Her ability to understand the punch line – in English – brought laughter comparable to a western child learning the joys of word play. (Grace is a great "room" for frustrated comedians, believe me: Pound for pound, the most giggles found on three continents.)

It was a great afternoon, shared by – among others – Diane McLaughlin, who was still being introduced to the orphanage complex that would become her home a few months later. McLaughlin would include "sea baths" as a healthy, fun, invigorating part of the Grace schedule. In time, the children grew confident in the water, came to terms with a tragedy and, not inconsiderably, learned they could have fun again.

The ocean remained a favorite destination, even after McLaughlin left the orphanage. Within hours of my arrival in February 2008, the girls quickly began asking, "Time for sea bath, Uncle?" They didn't have to strongly argue their case, and the first gap in our mutual schedules found us gathered at the beach.

Before unlocking the back gate, I made sure a proportionate number of the older girls – 16- and 17-year-olds – were on hand to help shepherd the soaking herd once we were in the ocean, along with staff to observe the big picture from the beach.

Out we dashed, across a short stretch of near-white sand to the lapping, dancing waves. The youngest children (never far from a matronly companion

Ocean view: In August 2005, visitors encouraged the Grace children for a "pool party" in the ocean (above), the first time the girls played in their beloved waves since the tsunami eight months earlier. (Below) Sometimes restful, other times troubled, the Indian Ocean provides the background for Grace Care Center.

from the Grace staff) settled in for a determined session of sand play, with small piles of packed dirt restricted only by the limits of imagination; groups of slightly older girls formed circles to sit and let the waves wash over them. Those in their teen years – who had long abandoned their fear of the water – took to the chest-high waves for some enthusiastic swimming.

I formed a line with the oldest girls, a human chain that marked the limits of the sea bath party. A symphony of sound blended the ocean's roar with children's laughter, accented with frequent shouts of "Uncle, Uncle" as they called for my attention: To be picked up, looked at, taken care of, loved.

Time melted away, the bright tropical sun bounced off the waves as the kids splashed each other. It was a workout for young and old, and, inevitably, we began directing the squealing hordes back to shore. I waited to work with the ebb and flow of the water from my "station," where I could no longer stand without being submerged.

The familiar call – "Uncle!" – took on a different tone; urgency and panic replacing playful attention-seeking. Two of the girls – 14, 15 years old – were struggling on a wave that climbed to considerable heights.

They'd been near the end of the line we'd formed, and slipped past me as the bouncing, rolling ocean took them further out to sea. Each round of waves heading toward the beach included a return trip out to sea, and the pull grew stronger the further from shore.

Although they were reasonable swimmers, that knowledge disappeared inside their fright as they felt carried away, further out to sea. They were panicking, screaming for their lives.

I plunged into the water toward them, fighting to ride a wave that would bring the girls close enough to grab. Someone produced a floating, circular toy that might help, and threw it towards the now-crying children, their voices rising in intensity with growing alarm. I reached and grabbed the first girl, encouraging her (later realizing that my English instructions meant little) to float with the water, not struggle. I held her and patiently eased us back toward shore, inch by inch until we caught the next inland-heading series of waves; I pushed her towards shore, and hoped that too much time hadn't passed.

Turning back, I saw that the other lost swimmer had been reached by three teenage boys, who were cooling off in the shallow water perhaps 100 meters up shore from us when our pool party began. (I'd noticed them edging closer to the impressive number of pretty young women, soon taking athletic dives or doing whatever else might warrant attention.) They weren't far behind me, and soon we were all accounted for on the beach.

I thanked the boys, profusely, for their help. They nodded humbly, modestly before heading back to their section of the beach. (They seemed disappointed that more time with the girls wasn't in the plan.) One of the two rescued girls was sick, and was held patiently while she coughed up the once-again threatening Indian Ocean. The Grace staff became a collective mother, taking the frightened children under their wing; admonishing them for swimming too far away from the others; loving them with gratitude for their safety.

That evening, I sat outside my room in the guest quarters, surrounded by rotating groups of children eager to try out a few English words, look at photos on a laptop computer, and spend time with their American visitor. Our nearly-lost little swimmers managed a smile after tearful apologies, and another day at Grace Care Center came to an end. From the perspective of a modest little porch, perhaps 100 meters from the shore, the waves were gentle and steady, an inconsistent ballet that found harmony with the surrounding sounds of nature, the winds lightly blowing through tropical leaves, the murmur of children's voices, and the squawking of crows taking the day's final flight above the beach.

At a distance, the ocean was a gentle invitation, an eternal neighbor with a history of nourishing a community, providing escape, and, sometimes, threatening the very existence of its people. Children would play in its waves, some eager, some timid; some with youthful innocence, other times with experienced wisdom. The ocean provided and took away, invited and rejected, and offered a timeless reflection of the delicate, fragile condition of survival.

That day, in northeast Sri Lanka, when peace seemed more elusive and unobtainable than ever, a minor victory, of sorts, was won. Another day ended without tragedy, offering teasing hopes that others might follow.

War is a battle you cannot win; If you win anything,
you will only make someone hate you.
Then there will be a day when they will win."
— Hiram Labrooy

Chapter 10

Starting Over ... Again

Not long after Eric Parkinson heard stories of the war in Trinco – described by Grace Care Center manager Diane McLaughlin and some young children – he received a report from Rev. Jeyanesan detailing the battle's byproducts. The shelling lasted a few weeks; recovery would take years.

"Greetings from St. John's, Grace Care Center and the field of battle," began Jeyanesan's August 17 2006 report to Parkinson and VeAhavta. "The situation is very bad now. Daily fighting is going on between the LTTE and the government forces." Rev. Jey spoke of refugee families with nowhere to turn; of civilians – including children – being killed; and of dwindling resources scrambling to provide relief and medical attention.

In Batticaloa, Jeyanesan, Rev. Earl P. Solomon, and a team of pastors and volunteers worked to deliver 19 trucks' worth of supplies to the Vaharai region, areas considered "uncleared" and – as with much of Batticaloa at the time – under control of the Tamil Tigers. The team obtained approval from local government officials to make the trip, although at the military checkpoint in Mankerni – just a few miles north of Batticaloa – they were stopped and held until evening, when they returned to St. John's without having completed their journey.

"We did not get the clearance to continue our mission," Jey said of the aborted deliveries of food and medicine.

"The one with the smile," was how visitors often described Tharshala Mahendran, a sweet, friendly child with a congenital heart defect. Diane McLaughlin and VeAhavta secured the contributions and services of doctors in Colombo to repair a hole that was discovered in the girls' heart, which threatened to take yet another young life.

They tried again, and – after the BBC reported the government's refusal to allow relief supplies to be delivered to those in need – continued with their efforts. The distribution of basic sustenance, Jey said, required a meeting with the Government Agent of Batticaloa and other officials from the district.

"We made all the arrangements and proceeded to Vaharai," Jey reported. "In all the checkpoints we were stopped, questioned and thoroughly searched. We were asked to unload half the items for checking, and had to reload them all." A half-hour mission turned into a four-hour ordeal before they made it to Vaharai, where 8,800 refugees had gathered. Families were afraid of staying in nearby buildings that might be targeted for an attack.

"In past battles," Jey said, "refugees who were sheltered in schools and other buildings were frequently killed in the shelling and bombing."

Instead, improvised camps were set up in barren fields or in smaller clusters along the road. Jeyanesan came upon one group of about 70 refugees, "Many of them ladies with small children, who cried and begged us to get them back to their communities," said Jeyanesan. "I spoke to a lady who delivered a baby at the road side two days earlier, the mother and child were still under a tree."

When the team arrived in Vaharai, they were gratified to serve people who came running to the trucks in search of food.

"After two weeks of starving, we were the first people to have reached them with relief items," said Jey. "We saw them cooking immediately after. We saw smiles on the faces of the kids and the people. This is the success of our mission and this is why our Almighty God has called us."

Not all of the news was as promising. The renewed conflict continued, and there were times when Jeyanesan listened to hours of shelling from an army camp less than four kilometers from St. John's, aimed at nearby Tiger-held compounds.

"At present, there are around 45,000 people displaced by the battle," Jeyanesan said in mid-August. Casualties continued in the aftermath of the heated exchange: Bodies were discovered along anonymous roadways, adding to the fatalities of the initial assaults. Help was needed, desperately, as Jey had underestimated the situation: More than 100,000 people in the eastern district were left without a home due to the renewed conflict. Jeyanesan joined the United Nations in declaring the situation a humanitarian crisis on par with what the tsunami left in its wake.

Numbers alone couldn't tell the full story. In many ways, the crisis was worse than what followed one of history's deadliest natural disasters: After the tsunami, recovery efforts benefited from the still-active cease-fire, the presence of the Sri Lanka Monitoring Mission, and a thriving community of international relief agencies who answered the tsunami's call. As a nation, Sri Lanka received billions of dollars in donated relief funds, and welcomed thousands of volunteers who launched projects in coastal communities.

Less than two years later, there were fewer resources to address a larger problem. The SLMM closed shop in Trincomalee, a decision made by most of the NGOs in the area. There were far fewer groups and individuals, working with fewer supplies and equipment, in an environment where the cease-fire was a truce in name only.

In America, Parkinson and VeAhavta volunteers launched a drive to quickly raise emergency funds. A modest goal of $15,000 was set – and met – to buy and distribute food, water, clothing and temporary shelter for as many people as possible. Parkinson promised prospective donors something that few NGOs could: "Every penny donated will go directly to Sri Lankan refugee relief," he said, a commitment fulfilled when he left California for yet another quickly-planned trip halfway around the world.

In some ways, the mission was comparable to the situation that first inspired Parkinson to establish Grace Care Center, a time when a blissful cease-fire seemed ready to allow for the daunting task of rebuilding the northeast. In other ways, the crisis rivaled that created by the tsunami, with shattered villages leaving inhabitants in search of basic shelter, provisions and hope.

This time, there were fewer people able – or willing – to help. Two

Supply and demand: As security increased, distribution in the northeast slowed as channels were frequently interrupted (above). Trucks often waited days before being cleared for travel. Army Major W.S.A. Wijetunge (below, center) helps distribute supplies near Batticaloa with Leonard David (right) and volunteers from St. John's. Wijetunge spoke with Eric Parkinson about possible relief projects near Trinco; a week later he was killed during combat in the north. (Photo by Sam Larkin.)

steps forward, two steps back, with fewer people making the journey.

After landing in Colombo, Parkinson and California volunteers Tori Wynn and Sam Larkin were greeted by Rev. Solomon, and went first to Batticaloa, where they joined the teams assembled by Rev. Jey and put the hastily-procured rations and supplies to work.

***

The intense periods of battle gave way to isolated, consistent attacks and counterattacks throughout the northeast. In early September, the Tigers publicly promised to keep government troops out of Sampur, a village enclave on the southern shore of the bay bordering Trincomalee. A week later, the LTTE retreated from Sampur, giving rise to speculation that the Tiger's numbers and strength were diminishing. The Christian Science Monitor observed that, in the two years since the cease-fire, the government had been able to replenish troops, supplies and strategy. The Tigers' ability to recruit lessened due to death, migration or a steady Tamil exodus from their country; those with means or resources were often choosing to leave Sri Lanka.

Along the east coast, Tiger-held communities near Batticaloa faced increasing threats from the LTTE-splinter group formed in 2004 by Vinayagamoorthi Muralitharan, a renegade Tiger known as Colonel Karuna who was, "Widely believed to have backing from the military," as the International Herald Tribune reported.

"The Karuna group is now in total control of rebel-held areas in eastern Ampara district," said group spokesman T. Thuyavan, amid allegations that Karuna soldiers were attacking Tiger troops, and that the Sri Lankan army was steadily extending north. Cease-fire monitors told the New York Times, "The truce now holds only on paper."

For a diplomatic solution, both sides claimed they were prepared to return to the negotiating table, yet discussion of a peaceful future would, if held, include questions about previous incidents. In the months since the cease-fire, more reports had surfaced about "disappearances," kidnappings by paramilitary organizations and (in unmarked white vans) by government agents; both sides were equally in search of fresh

Friends and neighbors: "All the money in the world won't float the boat; it's human relationships that will," said Eric Parkinson of his journey with VeAhavta and Grace Care Center. During a late 2006 visit, a ceremony at Grace (above) included Rev. S. Jeyanesan (second from left), Diane McLaughlin, Eric Parkinson and Father Lloyd Anthony Lorio. (Below) Parkinson at Grace with Leonard David from St. John's in Batticaloa, and Grace Care Center manager Rev. J. Gnanapragasm. (Photos by Sam Larkin.)

recruits or capturing potential enemies, and human rights agencies were asking questions.

Grace Care Center and Trincomalee settled into a post-battle prayer for normalcy, allowing themselves false hope whenever a day without a land – or nearby sea – clash again filled the air with the sounds of explosions. Amid the renewed conflict and subsequent emergencies, the collective heart of Grace Care Center and its many friends spent considerable time worried about the heart of an 11-year-old girl whose polite, quiet manner and infectious smile were threatened with the need for emergency surgery.

In late September, Tharshala Mahendran, a friendly newcomer to Grace Home who lost her father in the tsunami, received a troubling medical diagnosis. At school – where she hoped one day to become a teacher in those very classrooms – she complained of pains in her chest. An examination revealed a small hole in her heart, one that would require surgery if her life was to be saved.

Medical facilities in Trinco were not equipped for the necessary treatment and procedures. As with the Mercy Home elder Chandradasa ("Mr. Gandhi") when his aging heart began fading, Tharshala was sent to Colombo for further tests, a decision made uncertain of how treatments and surgeries would be paid for.

"She will have the surgery, the money will be found," declared Rev. Jeyanesan. Tharshala went to the nation's capital in the company of McLaughlin; plans were made in America for fund-raising activities to offset the cost of the medical care, although McLaughlin reported that it wouldn't be necessary. Dr. Shehan Perera told McLaughlin and Daisy Soundranayagam – a matronly addition to the orphanage staff as Program Director – that a source existed, a "Presidential fund," that would cover half the cost of the procedure. The balance, said the Singhalese doctor while preparing treatment for a young Tamil patient, would be waived. (McLaughlin said a "private, anonymous" donor who learned of Tharsala's situation paid the balance.)

First one surgery was conducted, during which it was discovered that the hole was larger than thought. Full open-heart surgery was performed, and declared a success.

"Once again, the good Lord is watching over our work,"McLaughlin said, describing the actions of a diverse medical crew as inspired by a generous deity, "Sharing his love with both Singhalese and Tamil doctors."

The news was relayed to friends in America and the staff at Grace, who in response told McLaughlin of night fire lighting up the Trincomalee sky at 4 a.m.; of gun boats floating on the bay; of helicopters overhead. For McLaughlin, the child's surgery was an obstacle that could be –and was – overcome. More threatening was the increased war, and questions that would soon decide her future in Sri Lanka.

The one-year anniversary of McLaughlin's tenure at Grace was coming to an end, the period an informal agreement with VeAhavta. Although she was paid a modest stipend for her service, costs had escalated and McLaughlin's financial resources had disappeared. Continuing at Grace was very much her heart's desire, but may not have been a practical expectation for the coming year.

Another consideration was even more personal, a life decision common to most people but, again, determined by the circumstances of Sri Lanka. Earlier that year, McLaughlin was introduced to Daisy Soundranayagam's nephew, a video producer and director named Jerome Lazarus. Although they were Tamil, Lazarus and his family felt safe in their Colombo neighborhood, with a solid circle of friends for which Singhalese, Tamil, or Muslim distinctions did not prevent good fellowship.

In spite of the challenges and escalating war, McLaughlin and Lazarus allowed themselves glimpses of hope. Their fast friendship turned romantic, and they discussed their prospects for a post-peace life, to include marriage, involvement with Grace and, perhaps, raising a family in Sri Lanka.

The summer's ongoing emergencies at Grace and uncertainty of war included drama both romantic and, at times, life-threatening. In late June 2006, Lazarus was in Colombo when he learned of the assassination of General Parami Kulatunga, deputy chief of staff and the third highest-ranking officer in Sri Lanka army. Kulatunga was en route to his office when an attack – which "bore the hallmarks of the Tamil Tigers," according to the New York Times – sent an explosives-carrying motorcycle crashing into his vehicle. Kulatunga was pronounced dead upon arrival at a Colombo hospital; four others were killed in the explosion, including a civilian and the bomber, and eight more were injured.

Security in the capital went to elevated status. By evening, when Lazarus was leaving work, the streets were well filled with police and military personnel. Lazarus saw a familiar face, a driver he knew in a military vehicle.

Lazarus asked what the panic was about. Rather than answer, the soldier demanded Lazarus' identity card and driver's license. The officers asked him questions: His name, occupation, and, "Are you Tamil?"

"I said yes, I am a Tamil," Lazarus said. They told him to put his identification on the hood of the vehicle. Hushed conversations were held, between police and soldiers from the nearby Army headquarters. Directors from Lazarus's office came to the scene to confirm his employment and schedule for that day (it was documented that Lazarus was nowhere in the vicinity of the morning's attack). The military said he could go free, but the police insisted that Lazarus be taken to their station for further questioning.

Although hesitant, Lazarus took the chance, gambled on his innocence.

"I said, fine, I don't want to make this situation bad," Lazarus said. "I went to the police station with my driver."

The outcome seemed pre-determined. Lazarus was questioned again, asked if he was Tamil. After saying 'yes,' he was taken into custody.

"Lock them up," Lazarus recalled hearing. "It was done, just like that."

He wasn't alone. Hundreds of Tamils were brought in for questioning that day. Personal belongings, cell phones, were taken. He wasn't allowed to contact anyone, but was told the next morning that his parents were informed of his location and situation.

"There was no dinner, no breakfast, we were just kept like that," Lazarus recalled. The police, again, took statements the next morning; fingerprints and photos were taken before the prisoners were driven to a court room. A group of Tamil men were taken before a judge, declared to be "under suspicion" of having worked with terrorists or having knowledge of terrorist activities. Each was told they would be held in custody for a minimum of seven days.

In a room estimated as 100 square feet, Lazarus said about 300 men and boys were kept. "It is like how you stuff sardines," he said of the cell, where men slept in the same clothes for days, lying on the ground. Some seemed to be on drugs, Lazarus noticed, wondering how their habits were fed in custody. (Others who have been in custody reported the availability of heroin and marijuana, sold by guards to inmates whose families brought rupees on the rare visiting opportunities.)

Lazarus was released after 10 days, accomplished through a lawyer friend of the family and sufficient bail money. Others weren't as fortunate, including two boys from Jaffna caught in the "round up" who were en route (with documentation) to a university in Great Britain, and others who remained in custody after Lazarus was freed.

"It is like a hell in there," Lazarus said. "I can't explain how bad it is. I thought of how I was going to live after that, how to face the situation. If people don't know the whole story, they might think I had been taken in for some other reason."

After his release, Lazarus reconsidered his options. Until being taken into custody, he believed he and his family were in good standing in their community. Following his incarceration, however brief, his confidence waned. For days he was unable to feel safe outside of his home, in the environment he thought he knew.

"I couldn't leave the house," Lazarus said. "When I passed a check point, my hands started shaking. I didn't want to go through that again."

Those were bitter days for Lazarus, who said, "I love Sri Lanka, and want to promote my country to the world," a mission he thought he could help achieve through his work. Instead, he now feared for his life. Those who complained were put at further risk: Lazarus spoke of people who filed official grievances over their treatment and were reportedly never heard from again.

Lazarus wondered about his future in Sri Lanka, as did McLaughlin. She felt the same "no-win" conflict heard from shopkeepers in Trinco, who were told by one group that they must obey a hartal and close their business; threatened by another that the shop would burn if it didn't remain open. McLaughlin was torn between her love for the children of Grace and the safety of a man with whom she believed she might have a future. There was no life for Lazarus in Colombo, let alone Trinco, and McLaughlin had few options beyond her one-year stay at Grace. For a while, she considered trying to find employment and a place to start a life with Lazarus (yet remain in contact with Grace).

"I've been looking at neighborhoods," McLaughlin said in November. "And nowhere is safe. They just had more roundups [in Colombo], the army came into all the houses, emptied every cabinet, pulled out drawers. How am I supposed to begin a life and, God willing, a family where you cannot move about freely?"

Opportunities to earn a living outside of Grace Care Center were limited. NGOs and relief agencies continued the mass-departure from Trinco that began with the shooting deaths of five students in January, and accelerated in the wake of the murders in Muttur. McLaughlin thought back on a year that began with her relocating to a disaster-torn, impoverished orphanage and ended in a conflict zone of increasing violence.

"I feel like I am living my life chapter by chapter, page by page," McLaughlin said in December. "The ups and downs; the thrills and spills; the war. I have no idea how it will end. It would be comforting to have a peek at the last few pages."

In spite of the overwhelming odds against hope, Eric Parkinson saw – as he had five years earlier when his odyssey began – possibilities within the challenges. Enemies were everywhere, but so were friends if viewed from the proper perspective. While distributing supplies in Batticaloa, Parkinson was joined by Sri Lankan Army Maj. W.S.A. Wijetunge, who held no motive other than basic humanity.

"He clearly had a genuine desire to help," Parkinson said, "and handed out packets to the predominantly Tamil people in the camp." Relief work is a great equalizer, and the day ended with a well-earned tea break, during which Parkinson learned that the 38-year-old Wijetunge was looking forward to some leave time he would soon be taking: He cherished the thought of time with his wife and two young children, who were about the same ages as Parkinson's son and daughter in California.

The men exchanged nods of universal, parental understanding. These children: you love them; worry about them. It's an international truth with little need for debate, and much to agree upon.

They spoke of other things, including a mobile clinic operation Parkinson and VeAhavta doctors were considering reviving. A pre-tsunami clinic successfully treated 10,000 patients during a marathon session; Wijetunge wanted to help restart the clinic, and was prepared to dedicate time to the project.

Parkinson thought of Wijetunge when, in Trincomalee, he continued making plans for what he considered the ultimate dream of Grace – a House of Peace Ecumenical (HOPE) Center that would allow and encourage religious study regardless of denomination, a path to a future Sri Lanka where various backgrounds could co-exist. Wijetunge, Parkinson thought, could help with that, or on other projects in the mixed-environment of Trinco.

Before Parkinson returned to the United States, he learned that Wijetunge was killed in a battle not far from the same refugee camp where he tried to help salvage lives destroyed by the war. Two more children left without a father.

Multi-ethnic and religious problems, Parkinson thought, were best solved by a diverse group of individuals with a common purpose. As usual, Parkinson's trip included the delivery of donations and supplies from various sources.

"The first time I went to Sri Lanka, I traveled alone and I carried three suitcases filled with donated medication," Parkinson said. Five years later, Parkinson again left the comfort of southern California armed with over-packed bags of cards, letters and photos for the children and elders, 100 donated backpacks, and what he called "life saving equipment," ring buoys, a rescue can and whistles suggested by VeAhavta volunteer Tom McLaughlin, a physical therapist, longtime water sports enthusiast and former lifeguard. During an August visit to Grace Home, Tom saw the children struggle against waves while taking their sea baths and the idea for the practical gifts was born.

Before leaving California, Parkinson also accepted a generous donation of $2,460 from the Islamic Society of San Luis Obispo. Parkinson was invited to speak at a local mosque, arranged by VeAhavta Chief Medical Officer, Dr. Rushdi Abdul-Cader. A week later, the mosque welcomed back their "Brother," and presented him with funds for refugee relief in Trincomalee and Batticaloa.

"This is remarkable," Parkinson said. "Not just because they called me a 'Brother,' but also because the check was made out to VeAhavta, an organization with a Hebrew name. This shatters the stereotypes about Muslims: They are not terrorists. They care deeply about others, even about people they don't know halfway around the world."

As promised, Parkinson was able to confirm the donations were delivered, and also to describe the unplanned benefits of how the Grace spirit can help Trinco – and Sri Lanka – heal its ethnic wounds. Parkinson smiled while the girls played little hostesses to children of all ethnic and religious backgrounds during an October ice cream social, a now regular event bringing together the Grace girls with Buddhist,

Hindu, Muslim and Christian orphans and students. "All of the children got along well and seemed to have a wonderful time playing in the park," Parkinson said. "The Grace girls made new friends."

Children are resilient, Parkinson saw, able to overcome their disappointment when an awards ceremony for a "net ball" tournament was canceled as blockades in the road made travel impossible. Security forces were defusing a claymore mine that was found in a shop not far from Grace Care Center while scattered battles took place nearby.

"Throughout the day we could hear the sound of mortar fire and rocket launches," Parkinson said. "The sounds were not loud, but they were fairly regular and served as a reminder of what was happening in the 'real world' outside the compound."

Near the end of his stay in Trinco, Parkinson arranged for a special celebration for the Grace girls, a "pool party" held at the Mauro Beach Hotel in Nilaveli; the same guest house Parkinson stayed at five years earlier while scouting locations for the orphanage. Parkinson often returned to that hotel; he toured its grounds in February 2005, just weeks after the tsunami tore down its walls and left a ruined courtyard in its wake. Now reopened, Parkinson rented the hotel's pool for an afternoon of splashing and playing with the Grace Home girls.

"The children – who had never been swimming in a pool before – had the facility to themselves," Parkinson said. "They had a blast." Some stayed in the shallow end, hesitant to venture too far too soon; others jumped without fear into the deeper water. The hotel manager opened the gate to allow access to both the beach and pool areas, and soft drinks and snacks were served on the patio. The manager was delighted with a "thank you song" performed by the children in Singhalese, in deference to their host.

Parkinson was proud of the girls for, "Doing their part to reach out to others across ethnic boundaries," a small slice of humanity in a nation that seemed, at times, irreparably torn.

The news reports volleyed between peace and war. In November, under international pressure, the Liberation Tigers of Tamil Eelam released 22 underage recruits to human rights agencies, claiming the children had lied about their ages in order to voluntarily join. Days later, 60 civilians were killed by artillery strikes in the eastern village Kithiraveli; men, women and children who had sought shelter from the war in an abandoned school. On Nov. 24, the Associated Press referred to the situation as an "undeclared civil war," one that escalated as tanks and warplanes attacked targets in Batticaloa. The government claimed they were ready to talk, while also promising to soon put an end to Tiger terrorism. By year's end, reports routinely included disclaimers that independent confirmation of government announcements could not be made, as travel to the north and east was severely restricted.

In late 2006, it briefly seemed that the conflict was fading after an explosive year of open warfare. On December 2 the International Herald Tribune observed that a suicide-bomb attack, intended to assassinate the younger brother of President Rajapakse, failed to complete its mission.

"A recent string of botched attempts … seems an unusual development," the Tribune reported. The government claimed that superior security measures were preventing additional deaths; some analysts said the Tiger numbers and ferocity were fading. News stories blurred the distinction between fact and fiction, reports ranged from the (confirmed) December 2006 arrest in London of Colonel Karuna, who was detained while traveling with a fake passport, to the often-reported (but never verified) speculation that Tiger head Velupillai Prabhakaran was dead.

In early 2007, however, the LTTE showed renewed power with aerial attacks. "The Tigers now have planes," Time magazine reported, a fleet of three, maybe four essentially hand-built aircraft were assembled in Jaffna, one smuggled piece at a time. The debut mission of the Air Tigers succeeded when they dropped bombs on oil fields near Colombo.

The war was approaching 25 years with little evidence of a conclusion being reached, or a solution being found.

After five years, Parkinson had made so many trips to Sri Lanka that the novelty had worn off, but never the charm, found in the smiling faces of children who no longer call him "Uncle," but "Eric-Appa," a father figure not above horsing around in a pool filled with children. On a tropical beach, beaming with the promise of paradise yet never far from the latest echo of war, Parkinson happily played with and listened to laughing girls, high, squeaky voices shrieking with delight. He played with them, talked to them, and looked in their eyes to see the unfairness of circumstance.

That's where the connection, as always, was made. In five years, the California attorney had met the gaze of many Sri Lankans: Children whose eyes reflected the glow of babies born into Western prosperity; prisoners who sacrificed their own safety so others may go free; a soldier trying to help the victims of the very war that killed him.

Against all odds, increasing costs, and ever-present danger, Grace Care Center remained a haven of more than just safety or nourishment for children and elders, but a small model of cooperation and connection that could, under the right circumstances, reveal the future of Trincomalee and Sri Lanka itself. Assistance, Parkinson learned, was about finding the right questions to ask, rather than assuming that outsiders brought ready-made answers to the table.

"It's about getting a foothold in the country and finding someone you can trust," Parkinson said. "Without that, it wouldn't go anywhere."

One on one, with children, clergy of all faiths, professionals or humble fishermen, Parkinson learned the value of looking into the eyes of others to find a reflection of hope, and trust. More financial resources had been spent by other agencies on other projects, but few resulted in the same sense of connection that Parkinson – and the volunteers of VeAhavta – developed over dozens of trips to Grace Care Center. The simple recognition that tells people they're not alone in their struggle, that someone cares about them, and worries about whether they live or die.

"The best thing we can do is form a community to reach out," Parkinson said. "All the money in the world won't float the boat. It's human relationships that will."

"And the ancient empty street's too dead for dreaming."
– "Mr. Tambourine Man," Bob Dylan

Final Encounters
Reminders and Other Observations

*My plane arrived just a few weeks after the Sri Lankan government
withdrew from the terms of the cease-fire agreement. That announcement, in
January 2008, was something of a formality: Since mid-2006, the truce had
been increasingly ignored; the pact was "threatened" scores of times, as reported
in the international press, and was a joke to those living in the country.*

*Hiram Labrooy and a hired driver met my flight after a long night's trip
from Trincomalee, the endless security checkpoints more than doubling the
time needed for the journey. Before heading out for Grace, we spent much of
the day in the nation's capital, maneuvering from zone to zone for supplies
that weren't available in the northeast.*

*Compared to previous visits, Colombo now made no secret of the nation's
"at war" status. The streets were decorated with billboards bearing images
of President Mahinda Rajapakse and slogans of promised victory. Oversize
maps illustrated which sections of the country were under LTTE control at
various times: The situation 10 years earlier; as it stood in early 2008; and
the forecast of Tiger elimination by the end of the year.*

*We headed for a shopping mall, a multi-leveled complex complete with
movie theater and food court. Western culture was present and accounted
for: The cinema showed "Alien vs. Predator;" restaurants included Pizza
Hut and KFC, with menus slightly adjusted for local tastes. Teenagers
roamed the corridors with a universal aimless quality while browsing cell
phones and DVDs.*

*On the whole, Colombo was another world compared to the Third World
poverty in Trinco, made all the more tragic considering how much better the*

south had fared than most of the north and east. Away from the capital's relative prosperity, post-tsunami recovery had not seen much progress.

The challenges facing Grace Care Center, Labrooy explained, were many, with dramatically rising costs due to the escalating war, and funding that struggled to keep pace. Many VeAhavta volunteers remained passionately committed to the cause, but western interest faded in the years since the disaster brought the island to international attention. Fewer people battled an even greater task. (The largely American supporters of VeAhavta – and other agencies – faced their own problems: Not long after the tsunami, disaster struck in New Orleans, demanding domestic attentions. A crippling economy in the years that followed left donors uncertain of their own financial security.)

Our shopping complete, we headed out for Trinco. By evening we were past Kandy, and a long day settled into a night's drive. In higher elevations, the modest road was little more than an unevenly carved interruption of jungle patches, open fields and, occasionally, small villages, where farmers and tradesmen gathered in the dim light of a roadside market.

Not far from a village quieted by nightfall, the first security checkpoint was on higher alert than I'd seen during earlier visits. We were met by rifle-ready troops flanking a military officer, who aimed a flashlight beam at me. The rear door was hoisted open; my bags were pulled to the ground, opened and searched. Our driver explained our destination; papers were reviewed and we were on our way. Three more similar stops were encountered that night.

The road seemed bumpier than I recalled (a memory that didn't exactly include a smooth ride). Occasional patches brought us to a near crawl through divots a foot or more deep. A particularly beaten section of road caught our driver off guard: We banged – hard – into a deep pothole, swung sharply to the left, and came to an abrupt halt in a shallow roadside ditch.

I had been in the rear seat of the van, and hadn't bothered with a safety belt. The slamming halt sent me flying toward the windshield; my fall was somewhat cushioned by the vacant, front passenger seat.

Labrooy, of course, thought my clumsy fall forward was hilarious, yet another source of the well-intended but often crude male-to-male exchanges

The Government of Sri Lanka placed this monument on a section of Batticaloa that, until the Army took control in late 2007, was "held" by the Liberation Tigers of Tamil Eelam. The battle for Batti was won by government forces, and was maintained by the TMVP, the ruling political party formed by members of the Tiger-renegade "Karuna" group.

we'd had since shortly after meeting one another. He said something about my, "Trying to grab hold" of him while falling forward; I noticed how often he seemed to think about one of us grabbing onto the other. We traded half-hearted, juvenile insults while taking a flashlight look at the front wheels. The damage was limited, and wouldn't prevent us from moving on.

We continued our pointless dialogue, held in a somewhat absurd situation. Making dumb jokes was a way of not thinking about the "bang" I heard when our tire hit that hole in the chewed-up road. Most of the recent damage, I learned, was from mortar fire. The sound when we hit the divot wasn't what I thought it was; there was no point imagining what it could have – might have – been.

***

The small room near the kitchen at Grace Care Center was quiet. My near-constant companion joined me while I ate a late breakfast: A sliced hard-boiled egg in a bed of vegetables wrapped in bread. I'd eaten the same meal a day or two earlier and remarked – within hearing range of the staff – how much I enjoyed it. At Grace, even the mildest indication you liked something ensured it would be offered on every possible occasion. It's that kind of place.

"These are really good," I said to my friend, a young lady who'd just turned 18. I asked her what the Tamil name would be for the meal (not that I could repeat it with any accuracy), and told her it might be called a "breakfast sandwich," on my side of the world. "Sort of like a Sri Lankan Egg McMuffin."

She smiled, at the tone more than the reference, and nodded without conviction.

"You have no idea what an Egg McMuffin is, do you?" She wasn't fully immune to the encroachments of western pop culture: I'd given her a "Harry Potter" book as a birthday present, as she was familiar with the young wizard, and Colombo included more than a few sightings of the restaurant chain's golden arches, but most of the indulgences in Sri Lanka's southeast may as well have been in Dubai as far as she was concerned.

"No, Uncle" she said, blushing a bit, shrugging. She seemed sad to admit that she hadn't been schooled in fast food advertisements as so many had, for so long, in so much of the world. Somewhere along the way the phrases and images became more than just a reflection of a culture, they somehow became the culture itself. I imagined telling an American teenager that someone their age didn't know the McDonald's menu as well as their own cell phone number; the response would likely be rolled eyes and gasping disbelief. I mean, like, how could someone not know that?

"Well, that's not necessarily a bad thing," I said. She smiled, blushed again, just a little. Her name was "Sundari." At least, that's what I called her when writing about the recruitment of child soldiers. Her childhood included time spent learning to shoot an AK-47 rifle, being trained by people who discussed – and carried out – suicide bomb attacks. Girls her age have been known to do that in Sri Lanka.

She's a terrific kid, Sundari, who I saw grow from rowdy "tom boy" into a beautiful young woman; smart, sweet, loving, she also had a wicked sense of humor, the potential for mischief, and a strong instinct for survival. She didn't want to wage war; she preferred to work for peace. I wrote about that, but couldn't use her real name without putting her in danger.

She was 15 when we met – just a few years after she spent time at a Tiger camp near Killinochchi. I went to Sri Lanka to learn – and write – about an orphanage that was recently blasted by a devastating natural disaster; instead I found war stories, some of which were told by children, both as survivors and participants.

Three years later, in February 2008, the tsunami seemed a distant memory. The results of some recovery work could be seen, although in lesser amounts in the northeast. The challenge of war, however, wasn't improving. The regional clashes in Muttur a year earlier were said to be finished when the government declared victory in the Eastern district, which was previously under LTTE control.

"Victory," however, didn't seem to bring many spoils to the northeast, which remained heavily populated with tsunami-responding camps for Internally Displaced Persons. Disaster reconstruction in the south and west

was said to be more than 90 percent complete by the end of 2007; supplies and donations for the northeast had accomplished less than 20 percent of the goals.

After finishing my Sri Lankan Egg McMuffin, we enjoyed – as became our habit – a relatively empty Grace Care Center. The children had already boarded the bus for their day at school. No longer a 'Grace Girl' attending the primary school, Sundari lived in the dorm for boarders at the Vocational Training School, and had free time before classes began; I was waiting for whatever was on that day's schedule. Usually we walked over to Mercy Home, wished the elders a good morning and waited for Labrooy to arrive. We talked about her plans, and what she would like to do when she left Grace. She wanted to teach: I thought she would make a fine educator, having watched her become a real leader to many of the younger girls.

I hoped she would have the chance to chase those dreams.

***

On my final morning in Trinco, Sundari and I were enjoying a game of Dom, a close relative of Checkers that she had taught me. Labrooy coached me on game techniques (although his "suggestions" somehow seemed to result in Sundari countering with a particularly decisive move on the board). We were joined by the elder men and women of Mercy Home, including Valliamma, one of the facility's first residents who shared with me her tragic tale of watching her son slaughtered by men in uniforms.

Prompted by Labrooy's attempt to sabotage my game, he and I continued our tradition of playful insults, using stories and incidents from our adventures of the past 10 days. The jokes became a competition, said with smiles. In universal "guy thing" tradition, we'd pull a fist back as if we planned to punch one another, each laughing at the obviously false attempt. Slapstick comedy knows no language barrier, and the elders and Mercy Home staff laughed as we joked with one another. (Sundari giggled hardest of all.)

Valliamma, however, didn't understand, and seemed to think I was truly preparing to hit our friend. She scolded me, with all the ferocity that a wagged finger and harsh word from a 60-pound elderly woman could muster. (Considerable, in other words: Few tongue-lashings are as severe as *those given by little old ladies.) She gave me quite a lecture before the others calmed her down – lovingly, yet amused over her confusion, knowing she could be excitable at times.*

Who was I, Valliamma asked, to think of harming Hiram Labrooy? He took care of everybody, and was there every day. Labrooy stayed with them, while visitors came and went, and usually didn't come back. Lately, there were fewer visitors and more departures.

Maybe she wasn't all that confused. The people in the seemingly forgotten northeast – regardless of ethnicity or religion – had long demonstrated a remarkable resiliency against challenges of every shape and source. In the years since the tsunami, that basic faith was put to test after test, leaving the region wondering if survival was still possible, and if anyone was going to help them. After 25 years of war, many Sri Lankans were beyond being scared or frightened; too many explosions in too few months left them numb to fear. They were often sad, sometimes angry, and – always – tired of the uncertainty: It's a weary life spent entirely in war, and a growing number of Sri Lankans define "peace" as something last seen before they were born.

From a military standpoint, armed conflict appeared ready to end – for now – with government troops seemingly successful in their mission. The 2007 victories in the Batticaloa District of the Eastern Province were followed by elections that placed members of the TMVP party in control. (The leadership of which reportedly includes soldiers from the breakaway "Karuna" group of dissatisfied Tigers, now aligned with the government.)

The momentum from eastern victories continued through 2008. Determined government troops marched on, pushing towards the Jaffna peninsula. In January 2009, the government claimed to have taken over the Tiger headquarters in Killinochchi, along with compounds – to include the air strips used by the LTTE's fledgling aerial branch – throughout Jaffna. Claims of "victory" were made, with justification that taking away the final strongholds of the Tigers would reduce them to, at best, scattered guerilla fighters scrambling from jungle camps. Statements were made that, once the war was behind them, the government and Tamil-interest political groups could work toward a peaceful future.

Country of contradiction: The conditions in Trincomalee (above), considered an improvement over much of the desperate poverty found in the northeast, are in stark contrast to (below) Kandy and other southern resort areas. By late 2007, tsunami reconstruction was estimated as being 90 percent complete in the southwest, but barely 20 percent accomplished in the north and east, the regions that took the brunt of the waves' destruction.

If this were a Hollywood (or, more appropriately, "Bollywood") movie, a classic "happy ending" could be written. There is evidence that such a conclusion could, some day, be recorded; testimony found in the tireless efforts of those who work to help others regardless of minor distinctions that overlook a common humanity. In a 'What if' frame of mind, I can picture the spirit of Grace Care Center growing in Trinco, joining forces with the many others doing similar work: A future in which the capable, willing and determined people are allowed to believe they will again, some day, know peace and opportunity.

I can't write that, not just yet. This isn't a movie or novel where heroics rule the day. I first went to Sri Lanka to document a community recovering from a natural disaster; the greater story was of a beaten country with an uncertain future. The reports were of individuals doing what they could – profiles in peace from a nation at war – to help provide hope. The "encounters" were mine, introductions to the people behind the statistics.

These reports, and encounters, reflect but a fraction of the brutality of life in northeast Sri Lanka. Each girl at Grace, elder of Mercy Home, fisherman, teacher, shopkeeper, farmer or taxi driver had a story to tell, of machete deaths and child soldiers, starving senior citizens and endless brutality, of rioting and war that create victims young and old.

The world should meet some of these children, and elders, and friends of Grace, perhaps get to know them as I have, watching the kids grow from stained innocence to teenagers with few options. Seemingly outnumbered, for every story of death and violence there are stories of selfless bravery, of human compassion and a genuine concern for the children. It might still be possible for the rest of the planet to get to know some of them, some day.

If they die young, however, they – and the world – will never get that chance.

State of Grace
Close Encounters in the Third World

"Everybody comes here looking for the same thing," Eric Parkinson said about Grace Care Center, a casual comment made during a casual moment at the orphanage. "They just don't know what it is until they see it."

When he first set foot on the seven beaten acres of beachfront property north of Trincomalee, Parkinson never expected Grace to remain such a fixture in his life. The idea was for VeAhavta to build a facility that, with the right combination of effort and timing, could become self-sufficient in a few years. At that point, he could, "Turn over the keys and go find something else to do."

It wasn't, of course, that easy. His first trip to Sri Lanka made him feel like, "A benevolent humanitarian coming to the aid of some poor, backward people," he said. "The relationship was unbalanced before it started: I felt I had everything to give, but nothing to receive. What could the people of Sri Lanka offer me?"

Plenty, as he and many others learned. No matter the changes to the nation – the situation going from bad to worse in the years since Grace opened – a sense of possibility remained, not because of money or funding, but from the connections made between the people of Trinco and their American friends.

"Hope is still alive," said Parkinson. "I have heard that hope in the voices of Rev. Jeyanesan and the children. Giving into despair is not an option. To give up would be to abandon our brothers and sisters – something we cannot do."

The founder of VeAhavta remains impressed: By the commitment of the group's volunteers; the connections made with the people at

Grace; and by the impact this sort of volunteer work (up close and personal) made on the lives of the visitors.

"VeAhavta is about combating poverty," Parkinson said, "but it's also about combating a different form of poverty. Philanthropy and volunteerism are good, but Sri Lankans are also filling a void in the souls of many Americans."

Over the years, visitors connected with the people of Grace, with each other, and with a place that offered what can only be described as a spiritual experience. "State of Grace" is the appropriate phrase.

"I cannot tell you how many people have come to me since this voyage began to 'confess' to me," Parkinson said. They went searching for answers they weren't aware needed asking. "It seems to bring up a lot of baggage for a lot of people, making them want to bare their souls. They think this kind of work may provide some sort of answer; and sometimes it does."

Parkinson himself felt a certain "deficit," he said, the lack of the community and village spirit found in abundance in Sri Lanka's suffering northeast.

"There's a certain deadness here in the United States that I don't see getting better any time soon. Like Martin Luther King said: 'The richer we become materially, the poorer we have become morally and spiritually.' This is the most amazing thing I have seen as a result of this walk. I thought I only had things to give and nothing to gain. I was so wrong. I've seen a culture; I've had a peek at a real village. It's made me feel my deficit very intensely. We have no more villages here in America, and it's killing us from the inside out."

For some, going to Grace was a reminder that hope can be found with the simplest human encounters. Justin Yax, an Ann Arbor doctor who helped conduct the first, pre-tsunami clinic operated out of Grace, said that he wasn't surprised that so many western visitors formed such close bonds with the people in Trinco.

"Life is not about what surrounds you, it's about who you're surrounded by," Yax said. "It's the quality of the people, of the souls

Prim and proper, yet capable of a girls' laugh on the cricket field, Sayanthini was among the more studious of the Grace girls. Afternoon games were often held outside of Mercy Home, with elder fans watching the children play.

Profiles in Peace: Physical therapist Tara Rondy walks with Kamalambigai during an August 2006 visit. (Below) University of Michigan student Alex Papo was the subject of approximately 100 "crushes" by the girls of Grace Home during his 2005 trip.

you're around. I think there are bad people, but there are also very good people. When you find them, hold on to them and never let them go. You're lucky to have found them."

The spirit is, particularly, found in the inexplicable atmosphere that separates Grace from its surrounding village, a "bubble" (as Diane McLaughlin called it during her tenure as manager) that protects the compound from the surrounding, harsher realities. There, but for the Grace, is not a pretty picture.

The connection that would be a long-term relationship often began early into the journey. Tom McLaughlin, a California physical therapist who later served on the VeAhavta Board of Directors, quickly understood that this was to be a sustained effort.

"Returning to Grace was what I promised myself I would do at the end of my first trip," said McLaughlin. "I was a sobbing mess upon departure (it was what some of the Grace girls remembered most about me!), and when the opportunity to go back came up, all my energy went into it."

Having seen Trinco in both war and peace, McLaughlin recalled being impressed by the resilient nature of not only the children, but the elders who turned Mercy Home into a viable community. He watched the children put their hearts and souls into a youth competition of singing, dancing and art; a contest held after they traveled seven sweltering hours in a bus to Batticaloa. He watched the Mercy Home residents, including one stooped woman at least in her 70s, tend the garden, "Like a 65-pound human roto-tiller," clearing the property of thorny plants one square yard at a time.

McLaughlin was among the group at Grace during the August 2006 battles surrounding Muttur, and learned that the children knew far more about the war and its impact than some visitors might think. After a, "Particularly concussive blast in close range," McLaughlin was approached by one of the Grace girls, a young teenager.

"She asked me if I was okay," McLaughlin said. "I believe she was half concerned for my comfort, and half embarrassed that her visitor

Originally from a poor, rural village in northern Sri Lanka, Kanustika would like to become a teacher, and enjoys reading books and telling stories to the younger girls at Grace Care Center.

has to endure the unrest. She feels an integral part of the events in her country, even responsible for them as my host."

The feeling about Grace hardly diminishes with familiarity. Also at the orphanage during the Muttur shelling was Cheryl Huckins, Mercy Home co-planner who (as of August 2008) made four trips to Trinco; the thought of a fifth is never far from her mind.

"It was like returning to summer camp," she said. "An odd comparison, given the circumstance, but it is akin to returning someplace very special, which has many memories and intense relationships developed in a short period of time."

Huckins, as many have felt, said that the simple pleasures are, perhaps, easiest to appreciate, a feeling all the more pronounced during the height of war.

"You learn to relish the details of everyday life, Huckins said. "The world outside was going crazy, and impacted what we could and couldn't do, but on campus I felt like things were more 'real,' that there weren't layers of politics and agendas that were unspoken and that I couldn't understand. It felt more like returning to a second home – you pick up where you left off, do what you can, and hopefully leave it a little better off. And, enjoy the journey."

It's the best kind of journey, the volunteers said, where more can be learned by asking questions than pretending to have all the answers.

***

The first time I "returned" to Grace, I felt that, if I'd had a boyhood dog, it would have come running out of the children's garden to greet me, happily barking with tail wagging. As I've said, it's that kind of place.

My knowledge of Sri Lanka was (very) limited when I first heard of the tsunami, when I learned about Grace Care Center, an orphanage that could use a little help.

Things change, quickly. Within a few weeks of becoming aware of a place called Trincomalee, I boarded a plane with a group of strangers, some of whom are now among my closest friends. I had no idea what to expect, either of the country or the orphanage.

Known as "the baby" when she first came to Grace at age 6, Ramesh Dachayani was more interested in the beach than the water during a "sea bath" in August 2006.

It was nothing like I imagined; yet felt so very familiar. It would take more than a brief introduction to understand the story – the many, many stories – of Sri Lanka, yet the tale was easily understood from the perspective of Grace's seven peaceful acres. Within the orphanage walls are the survivors of war and poverty; the future of the children is the destiny of the nation, the haunting memories of the elders is the history of a culture. Outside of Grace is a multi-layered, generations-long political and ethnic riddle to be solved: The answer will come from the connections people make with one another.

The volunteers have learned that lesson, these friends of VeAhavta and the Grace Care Center. Diane McLaughlin spent an incredible – at times dangerous – year at the orphanage, leaving the country under circumstances beyond her control, with a husband and a lifelong commitment that may one day be renewed in person.

As with many others who traveled to Grace – before the tsunami, after the disaster or in the years since while a reignited war took over the island – life-altering plans will likely be made in the years ahead. There are hopes that the end of armed conflict could lead to a civil rights movement for Tamils, Muslims and other minorities. Many Sri Lankans, and others around the world, hope to see the international community help facilitate this effort, yet the small island's isolated place on the map (other than proximity to India) doesn't threaten any neighboring countries, and the interests of the world are usually captured out of defensiveness or commerce rather than simple humanity. (The same byproduct of geography leaves those who would seek escape from Sri Lanka with few options.)

What began as a journalist's report has, obviously, become a personal concern. On my first morning in Trincomalee, I rode in a tuk-tuk along a small path bordering a modest village. Coming up the trail was a young girl, perhaps 8 or 9 years old, walking with the bouncing step unique to children, carrying a few slim books. Her eyes were fixated on a spot on the ground just a few feet ahead of her; she seemed to be thinking about nothing in particular. She suddenly began skipping, doing a happy jump or two before continuing at a satisfied pace.

I never saw that child again. I kept going back, hoping to see more kids skipping down a road for no apparent reason.

To learn about VeAhavta, please visit www.you-shall-love.com

Assorted sources
Selected Bibliography

Portions of chapters 1 and 2 were drawn from articles published in *The Humanist* magazine: "Grace and Goodwill: The Ballad of Eric-Uncle and Rev. Jey," May/June 2007; and "Soldier Girl? Not Every Tamil Teen Wants to be a Tiger," September/October 2006, copyright © James A. Mitchell.

The author would like to acknowledge news agencies including The International Herald Tribune, the New York Times, the BBC, Reuter's and the Associated Press. For matters of known fact, specific attribution is not included where confirmation was made from two or more sources. Unless otherwise noted, individual comments were from interviews conducted by the author or correspondence with those cited. The author would again like to express his appreciation to those who gave their time to this project.

Other sources consulted for specific incidents or facts include:
Articles:
"Senior Sri Lanka minister killed," BBC News, Aug. 13, 2005
"Civil War looms in a divided nation," by Peter Foster, Gulf News, Aug. 17, 2005
"S. Lanka to probe youth deaths over execution report," by Ranga Sirilal, Reuters, Jan. 4, 2006
"Deadly attack on Sri Lanka navy," CNN, Jan. 7, 2006
"Sri Lanka raid sparks fishing ban," BBC News, Jan. 8, 2006
"Sri Lanka violence rises," by Peter Apps, Reuters, April 12, 2006
"Mediators scramble to save Sri Lanka peace talks," by Shimali Senanayake, New York Times, April 18, 2006
"People flee Sri Lanka port town," by Dumeetha Luthra, BBC News, April 29, 2006

"Killing of Trincomalee Tamil youths: Will justice be done?" by D.B.S. Jeyaraj, Sunday Leader, May, 2006,

"Sri Lanka's war in all but name," by Paul Danahar, BBC News, May 12, 2006

"Sri Lankan city mired in ethnic violence," New York Times, by Somini Sengupta, May 15, 2006

"Stop war 'in the name of the children,'" BBCSinhala.com, by Sarol Pathirana, May 28, 2006

"Former Sri Lanka rebels recruit child soldiers – UN" Reuters, June 22, 2006

"Sri Lanka bombs rebels after bus blast kills 61," by Peter Apps, Reuters, June 15, 2006

Sri Lankan General's killing points to rebels, monitors say," by Shimali Senanayake, New York Times, June 26, 2006

"Setting the straights for safety," by Dushiyanthini Kanagasabapathipillai, BBC, July 27, 2006

"Sri Lanka rebels say war back on," by Simon Gardner, Reuters, July 31, 2006

"Muslims flee Sri Lanka fighting," BBC News, Aug. 2, 2006

"Sri Lanka fighting rages," by Peter Apps, Reuters, Aug. 3, 2006

"The Sri Lankan town that rarely smiles," by Tom Whipple, Timesonline (UK), Aug. 3, 2006

"Sri Lanka blast kills bodyguard and a 3-year-old," by Shimali Senanayake and Somini Sengupta, New York Times, Aug. 9, 2006

"Two more slain aid workers found in Sri Lanka," International Herald Tribune, Aug. 8, 2006

"Families tell of Sri Lanka aid staff's final hours," by Peter Apps, Reuters, Aug. 8, 2006

"Sri Lanka rebels say army offensive kills 50 civilians," by Peter Apps, Reuters, Aug. 10, 2006

"Monitors say troops killed air workers in Sri Lanka," by Shimali Senanayake and Somini Sengupta, New York Times, Aug. 31, 2006

"Sri Lanka battles a weakened Tamil Tigers," by Anuj Chopra, Christian Science Monitor, Sept. 5, 2006

"Sri Lanka's rival rebel groups battle over territory in the east," International Herald Tribune, Sept. 6, 2006

"28 Killed as Sri Lankan Army breaches rebels' front lines," by Shimali Senanayake, New York Times, Sept. 11, 2006

"Kidnappings haunt long war in Sri Lanka," by Somini Sengupta, New York Times, Nov. 7, 2006

"Tamil Tigers say military killed 60 civilians," Associated Press, Nov. 9, 2006

"Failed suicide attack unusual for Sri Lankan rebels known for precision," Associated Press, Dec. 2, 2006

"Sri Lanka says revels shell school, wound students," by Simon Gardner, Reuters, Dec. 7, 2006

"UN fears for Sri Lanka civilians," BBC News, Dec. 12, 2006

"Sri Lanka helicopter gunships fire rockets at rebels," by Ranga Sirilal, Reuters, Feb. 6, 2007

"Tamil Tigers bomb Sri Lankan fuel facilities," Associated Press, April 28, 2007

"U.S. concerned at Sri Lanka abuses, halts some aid," New York Times, May 10, 2007

"Military: Troops capture last Tamil Tiger rebel base in volatile east," Associated Press, July 11, 2007

"Analysis: Sri Lanka war, humanitarian crisis to grind on," by Peter Apps, Reuters, July 19, 2007

"Sri Lanka rules out UN human rights observer mission amid charges of rights violations," Associated Press, Aug. 7, 2007

"Report blames forces in Sri Lanka aid massacre," by Peter Apps, Reuters, April 1, 2008

Assorted reports:

"The Voices of Girl Child Soldiers, Sri Lanka," by Yvonne Keairns, PhD, 2003, Quaker United Nations Office

"What happened to young people of Sri Lanka" – Nov. 2005, The Lanka Academic, by Dr. Charuni Senanayake

Amnesty International Report, 2007: Sri Lanka

"Death Threats in Trinco," Urgent Action Appeal from Amnesty International, May 3, 2008

Books (for consultation, confirmation or inspiration):

"Ethnic Warfare in Sri Lanka," by William Clarance, 2007, Pluto Press

"Sri Lanka in the Modern Age," Nira Wickramasinghe, 2006, University of Hawaii Press

"Ceylon," S. A. Pakeman, 1964, Frederick A. Praeger

"India and South Asia: A Short History," David Ludden, 2002, Oneworld Publications

"The States of South India," edited by A. Jeyaratnam Wilson and Dennis Dalton, 1982, C. Hurst & Co.

"Ceylon: A Divided Nation," B. H. Farmer, 1963, Oxford University Press

"Images of Sri Lanka Through American Eyes," H.A.I. Goonetileke, 1976, U.S. Information Service

"The Reefs of Taprobane," Arthur C. Clarke, 1956, Harper & Brother

Legal Matters

- All photos by James A. Mitchell unless otherwise noted. The author appreciates use of photographs taken or contributed by Eric Parkinson, Naresh Gunaratnam, Hiram Labrooy, Fr. Lloyd Anthony Lorio, Sam Larkin, Lynn Helland and Erin Whaley.

- The author gratefully acknowledges the following artists and companies for allowing use of lyrics from the following songs:

"Who'll Stop the Rain," written by John C. Fogerty, courtesy of Concord Music Group, Inc.

"Mr. Tambourine Man," written by Bob Dylan, copyright © 1964; renewed 1992 Special Rider Music. All rights reserved. International copyright secured. Reprinted by permission.

"Gimme Shelter," Words and music by Mick Jagger and Keith Richards, © 1969 (Renewed) ABKCO Music, Inc., All rights reserved. Used by permission from Alfred Publishing Co., Inc.

"You Can Call Me Al," copyright © 1986 Paul Simon, Used by permission of the Publisher, Paul Simon Music.

About the Author

A native of southeast Michigan, James A. Mitchell is the author of *It Was All Right: Mitch Ryder's Life in Music,* the career biography of the Detroit Wheels singer and voice behind "Devil With a Blue Dress On," and of *Applegate: Freedom of the Press in a Small Town,* based upon his experiences at a rural weekly newspaper.

Mitchell is a veteran of the U.S. Army, survivor of 10 years of living and working in New York City, and communications director for VeAhavta, the nonprofit organization responsible for the Grace Care Center orphanage and elder's home in Trincomalee, Sri Lanka.

During his first trip to Sri Lanka in February 2005, author James A. Mitchell was a frequent visitor to an Internet store in Trinco. Three years later, Buddhist monk Kamamaldeniye Pamgnabissa said he recalled seeing around town the "white man wearing a hat" not long after the tsunami. (Photo by Lynn Helland.)

Index

CPSIA information can be obtained at www.ICGtesting.com
Printed in the USA
BVOW04s0617220514

354163BV00009BB/899/P

9 781905 021116